SUPREME COURT OF INDIA'S LEADING CASE LAWS ON
INSOLVENCY AND BANKRUPTCY CODE 2016

CASE NOTES - FACTS - FINDINGS OF APEX COURT JUDGES - CITATIONS

JAYPRAKASH BANSILAL SOMANI
ADVOCATE, SUPREME COURT OF INDIA

INDIA • SINGAPORE • MALAYSIA

Notion Press

No.8, 3rd Cross Street,
CIT Colony, Mylapore,
Chennai, Tamil Nadu – 600004

First Published by Notion Press 2020
Copyright © Jayprakash Bansilal Somani 2020
All Rights Reserved.

ISBN 978-1-63633-508-7

This book has been published with all efforts taken to make the material error-free after the consent of the author. However, the author and the publisher do not assume and hereby disclaim any liability to any party for any loss, damage, or disruption caused by errors or omissions, whether such errors or omissions result from negligence, accident, or any other cause.

While every effort has been made to avoid any mistake or omission, this publication is being sold on the condition and understanding that neither the author nor the publishers or printers would be liable in any manner to any person by reason of any mistake or omission in this publication or for any action taken or omitted to be taken or advice rendered or accepted on the basis of this work. For any defect in printing or binding the publishers will be liable only to replace the defective copy by another copy of this work then available.

Dedicated

To

All the Past and Present Judges of the Supreme Court of India.

Salute to their wisdom.

Salute to their interpretation of Law.

Salute to their elaborative judgement writing skills.

Contents

Best Wishes to This Book From…..   13

Preface   19

1. Innoventive Industries Ltd. vs. ICICI Bank and Ors. (31.08.2017 – SC)   21
   - Insolvency And Bankruptcy Code, 2016 - Section 13; Section 14; Section 238; & Maharashtra Relief Undertakings (Special Provisions Act), 1958 - Section 4

2. Surendra Trading Company vs. Juggilal Kamlapat Jute Mills Company Ltd. and Ors. (19.09.2017 – SC)   25
   - Sections 7(5),9(5) and 10(4) of Insolvency and Bankruptcy Code, 2016

3. Mobilox Innovations Private Limited vs. Kirusa Software Private Limited (21.09.2017 – SC)   29
   - Sections 8 and 9 of Insolvency and Bankruptcy Code, 2016 & Legislative Guide on Insolvency Law of the United Nations Commission on International Trade Law

4. Macquarie Bank Limited vs. Shilpi Cable Technologies Ltd. (15.12.2017 - SC)   32
   - Section 9(3)(c) of Insolvency and Bankruptcy Code, 2016

Contents

5. Bank of New York Mellon, London Branch
   vs. Zenith Infotech Limited (21.02.2017 – SC)   35
   - Section 3(e) , 3(f) and Section 15 of the SICA & Section 252 of Insolvency and Bankruptcy Code, 2016

6. Anuj Jain vs. Axis Bank Limited and Ors. (26.02.2020 – SC)   40
   - Sections 3(10), 5, 5(7), 5(8), 43, 43(4), 44, 45 and 66 of Insolvency and Bankruptcy Code, 2016

7. ArcelorMittal India Private Limited vs.
   Satish Kumar Gupta and Ors. (04.10.2018 – SC)   44
   - Section 29A of Insolvency and Bankruptcy Code, 2016

8. Vijay Kumar Jain vs. Standard Chartered Bank and Ors.
   (31.01.2019 – SC)   49
   - Section 5, Section 21, Section 24, Section 25, Section 29, Section 30 & Section 31 of Insolvency and Bankruptcy Code, 2016

9. K. Sashidhar vs. Indian Overseas Bank and Ors.
   (05.02.2019 – SC)   54
   - Section 33 & Section 34 of Insolvency and Bankruptcy Code, 2016

10. Embassy Property Developments Pvt. Ltd. vs. State of
    Karnataka and Ors. (03.12.2019 – SC)   63
    - Sections 6, 7, 61 and 65(1) of Insolvency and Bankruptcy Code, 2016

11. Maharashtra Seamless Limited
    vs. Padmanabhan Venkatesh and Ors. (22.01.2020 – SC)   67
    - Insolvency And Bankruptcy Code, 2016 - Section 12-A

Contents

12. Duncans Industries Ltd.
    vs. A.J. Agrochem (04.10.2019 – SC)   70

    ♦ Insolvency And Bankruptcy Code, 2016 - Section 9;
    Tea Act, 1953 - Section 16G(1)(c)

13. Municipal Corporation of Greater Mumbai (MCGM)
    vs. Abhilash Lal and Ors. (15.11.2019 – SC)   74

    ♦ Insolvency And Bankruptcy Code, 2016 - Section 238;
    Mumbai Municipal Corporation Act, 1888 - Section 92; Section 92A

14. Jaiprakash Associates Ltd. and Ors. vs. IDBI Bank Ltd.
    and Ors. (06.11.2019 – SC)   78

    ♦ Insolvency And Bankruptcy Code, 2016 - Section 29A

15. Anand Rao Korada vs. Varsha Fabrics (P) Ltd. and Ors.
    (18.11.2019 – SC)   82

    ♦ Insolvency And Bankruptcy Code, 2016 - Section 231;
    Section 238

16. Jignesh Shah and Ors. vs. Union of India (UOI) and Ors.
    (25.09.2019 – SC)   85

    ♦ Companies Act, 1956 - Section 433; - Section 434;
    Insolvency And Bankruptcy Code, 2016 - Section 7

17. Rajendra k. Bhutta vs. Maharashtra Housing and Area
    Development Authority and Ors. (19.02.2020 – SC)   90

    ♦ Insolvency And Bankruptcy Code, 2016 - Section 14(1)(d)

18. Rahul Jain vs. Rave Scans Pvt. Ltd.
    and Ors. (08.11.2019 – SC)   94

    ♦ Insolvency And Bankruptcy Code, 2016 - Section 30

19. B. K. Educational Services Private Limited vs.
    Parag Gupta and Associates (11.10.2018 – SC)   96

    ♦ Sections 7 and 9 of Insolvency and Bankruptcy Code,
      2016 & Limitation Act

20. State Bank of India vs.
    V. Ramakrishnan and Ors. (14.08.2018 – SC)   100

    ♦ Sections 14, 60(2),96 and 101 of Insolvency and
      Bankruptcy Code, 2016

21. Transmission Corporation of
    Andhra Pradesh Limited vs. Equipment Conductors
    and Cables Limited (23.10.2018 – SC)   103

    ♦ Section 9 of Insolvency and Bankruptcy Code, 2016

22. Reliance Communication Limited and Ors. vs.
    State Bank of India and Ors. (20.02.2019 – SC)   106

    ♦ Contempt Of Courts Act, 1971 - Section 12(4),
      Insolvency and Bankruptcy Code, 2016 - Section 9;
      Constitution of India - Article 142

23. Jaipur Metals and Electricals Employees Organization
    vs. Jaipur Metals and Electricals Ltd. and
    Ors. (12.12.2018 – SC)   109

    ♦ Sick Industrial Companies (Special Provisions) Act,
      1985 [Repealed] - Section 20; Companies Act, 2013
      - Section 419(4), Section 434, Section 434(1); Section
      10E(1), Insolvency and Bankruptcy Code, 2016 -
      Section 7, Section 8, Section 9, Section 14, Section 238,
      Section 239, Section 255

24. Forech India Ltd. vs. Edelweiss Assets Reconstruction
    Co. Ltd. (22.01.2019 – SC)   114

    ♦ Sick Industrial Companies (Special Provisions) Act,
      1985 [Repealed] - Section 20; Companies Act, 2013 -
      Section 419(4), Section 434, Section 434(1); Insolvency
      and Bankruptcy Code, 2016 - Section 9; Section 10

Contents

25. K. Kishan vs. Vijay Nirman Company Pvt. Ltd.
    (14.08.2018 – SC)   117

    ♦ Arbitration and Conciliation Act, 1996 - Section 4, Section 9, Section 9(5), Section 34, Section 34(3), Section 37; Limitation Act, 1963 - Section 14; Insolvency and Bankruptcy Code, 2016 - Section 2, Section 3(11), Section 8, Section 8(1), Section 8(2), Section 9, Section 9(2), Section 9(5), Section 238; Insolvency and Bankruptcy (Application to Adjudicating Authority) Rules, 2016 - Rule 98(2)

26. Babulal Vardharji Gurjar vs. Veer Gurjar Aluminium Industries Pvt. Ltd. and Ors. (14.08.2020 – SC)   120

    ♦ Insolvency And Bankruptcy Code, 2016 - Section 7

27. JK Jute Mill Mazdoor Morcha vs. Juggilal Kamlapat Jute Mills Company Ltd. and Ors. (30.04.2019 – SC)   125

    ♦ Insolvency And Bankruptcy Code, 2016 - Section 3(23); Section 5(20); - Section 5(21); Trade Unions Act, 1926 - Section 2(h); Section 2(g); Trade Unions Act, 1926 - Section 8; Section 13; Section 15(c); Section 15(d)

28. Vinay Kumar Mittal and Ors. vs. Dewan Housing Finance Corporation Ltd. and Ors. (31.01.2020 – SC)   128

    ♦ Insolvency And Bankruptcy (insolvency And Liquidation Proceedings Of Financial Service Providers And Application To Adjudicating Authority) Rules, 2019 - Rule 5, Rule 6; Insolvency and Bankruptcy Board of India (Insolvency Resolution Process for Corporate Persons) Regulations, 2016 - Regulation 6; Insolvency And Bankruptcy Code, 2016 - Section 14, Section 15, Section 21(6A), Section 227, Section 239(2); National Housing Bank Act, 1987 - Section 36, Section 36(A)

29. Swaraj Infrastructure Pvt. Ltd. vs. Kotak Mahindra Bank Ltd. (29.01.2019 – SC)   131

- Recovery of Debts Due to Banks and Financial Institutions Act, 1993 - Section 17; - Section 18; Companies Act, 1956 - Section 434(1)(b), Insolvency and Bankruptcy Code, 2016; Constitution of India - Article 226, Constitution of India - Article 227

30. State Bank of India vs. Jah Developers Pvt. Ltd. and Ors. (08.05.2019 – SC)   134

- Advocate Act, 1961 - Section 30, Arbitration Act, 1940, Constitution Of India - Article 19(1), Article 21, Article 22(3), Article 136, Article 136(1), Industrial Disputes Act, 1947 - Section 10A, Section 21, Section 22, Insolvency And Bankruptcy Code, 2016 - Section 29A, Punjab Welfare Officers Recruitment and Conditions of Service Rules, 1952 - Rule 6(6), Railway Protection Force Rules, 1987 - Rule 153.8

31. Swiss Ribbons Pvt. Ltd. and Ors. vs. Union of India (UOI) and Ors. (25.01.2019 – SC)   138

- Sections 12A, 29A, 240A, 60, 53, 30 and 31 of Insolvency and Bankruptcy Code, 2016 [Code], Article 14 of Constitution of India and Section 433(e) of Companies Act, 1956

32. Pioneer Urban Land and Infrastructure Limited and Ors. vs. Union of India (UOI) and Ors. (09.08.2019 – SC)   148

- Constitution Of India - Article 14; Article 19(1)(g); Article 300-A; Article 19(6) & Sections 5 and 7 of Insolvency and Bankruptcy Code, 2016

Contents

33. Rojer Mathew vs. South Indian Bank Ltd. and Ors. (13.11.2019 – SC)   155

  ♦ Constitution Of India - Article 110; Constitution Of India - Article 323-A; Constitution Of India - Article 323-B; Finance Act, 2017 - Section 184, Insolvency And Bankruptcy Code, 2016 - Section 62, Section 182;

34. LMJ International Ltd. and Ors. vs. Sleepwell Industries Co. Ltd. (20.02.2019 – SC)   169

  ♦ Arbitration And Conciliation Act, 1996 - Section 49; Section 48 , Insolvency and Bankruptcy Code, 2016 - Section 10

35. Standard Chartered Bank vs. MSTC Limited (21.01.2020 – SC)   172

  ♦ Recovery Of Debts And Bankruptcy, Insolvency Resolution And Bankruptcy Of Individuals And Partnership Firms Act, 1993 - Section 22(2)(e)

36. List of some important videos and TV shows on Law & EXIM by Adv. Jayprakash Somani on his YouTube Channel 'jaysomani64'   175

  ♦ IBC, Bail, Supreme Court Jurisdictions, Writ Petition, PIL, SLP & many other videos on Law & Import Export Business.

Synopsis   *175*

List of some important videos & TV shows on Law & Exim by Adv. Jayprakash Somani on his YouTube Channel 'jaysomani64'   *177*

List of Adv. Jayprakash Somani's upcoming books   *181*

Best Wishes to This Book From.....

Jeetender Gupta
Advocate on Record
Supreme Court of India

Girdhar Govind,
Advocate, Supreme Court of India

Ravinder Nath Kansal
Advocate, District Courts, Faridabad.

P K Sachdeva
Advocate NCLT, NCLAT, DRT, DRAT etc.

Hari Subramaniam
Patent Attorney, Former President, Asian Patent Attorneys Association, India Chapter.

T Sundar Ramanathan
Advocate on Record, Supreme Court of India

M M Sharma
Advocate
Head- Competition Law Practice
Vaish Associates Advocates

Yuvraj Baburao Gaikwad
Advocate, Supreme Court of India

Prashant Shantaram Chaudhari
Advocate, Supreme Court of India

Dr. R. R. Deshpande
Advocate, Supreme Court of India

Best Wishes to This Book From…..

Atul Dakh
Advocate, Supreme Court of India

Ambuj Agarwal
Advocate, Supreme court of India

Shirish Deshpande
Advocate, Supreme Court of India

Ravi Pagare
Advocate, Supreme court of India

Rajnishkumar Sharma
Advocate, Supreme Court of India

Mahesh Zanwar
Advocate, High Court of Bombay, Mumbai

Madan Vaishnawa
FCA ACS and insolvency professional, Mumbai

Aditi P. Deshpande
Advocate, Supreme court of India

Nishit Dave
Dushyant Dave
Decode IPE , Mumbai

Vijay Shankar Khamkar
Advocate, Supreme court of India

A. K. Acharyya
Advocate, High Court Calcutta

Umesh Chand Goyal
Insolvency Professional, Delhi

R R Bag
Advocate, Supreme court of India

M. Ramalingam
FCMA, MBA, IP (
AGM (Retd) APSFC),
Visakhapatnam, Andhra Pradesh

Best Wishes to This Book From…..

Selvarajan Chokkan

B.Sc, CAIIB, Adv Wealth Mgmt (IIBF) Insolvency Professional (Regd) CM SBI

K Vatsa Kumar

BE , MBA , CAIIB & Insolvency Professional

K Ganesan

B.Com., CAIIB, Asst. General Manager (VRS), Indian Bank / Insolvency Professional

Pradeep Goyal

Insolvency Professional, Delhi

Rajeev Dhingra

CA, IP, RV (SFA), ID, Delhi

Chinna Gurappa

M Com, FCMA and IP.

Justice Lalit Kumar Mishra

Advocate, Supreme Court India (Former Judge, Orissa High Court)

Shobha J. Somani

Advocate, Family Court & District Court, Pune

Pankaj Joshi

Advocate, Supreme Court of India

Divyansh Rai

Advocate, Supreme Court of India

Pawan Shukla

Advocate, Supreme Court of India

Vijay Verma

Advocate, Supreme Court of India

Rohit Singh Rajawat

Advocate, Supreme Court of India

Lokesh Kumar Choudhary,

Advocate On Record, Supreme Court of India

Best Wishes to This Book From.....

Asish Sarkar

Advocate, Supreme Court of India

Tejasvi Goel

Advocate, Supreme Court of India

Gobind Kumar

Advocate, Supreme Court of India

Kailas Udhavrao More

Advocate, Supreme Court of India

Javed S. K.

Advocate, Supreme Court of India

Vivek Solshe

Advocate, Supreme Court of India

Deepa Kulkarni

Advocate, Supreme Court of India

Aphzal Ansari

Advocate, Supreme Court of India

Sanjay Kustwar

Advocate, Supreme Court of India

Sreeramulu Badam

Advocate and Former Assistant Government Pleader in the High Court of Andhra Pradesh

Bhagyoday Mishra

Advocate, Gujrat High Court

Pramodkumar Ladda

CS & Insolvency Professional, Pune

Sandeep Gupta

Insolvency Professional, Delhi

Dendukuri Zitendra Rao

Cost Accountant & IP, Hyderabad

Best Wishes to This Book From…..

Keshav Rambhau Chinchwade

CA, IP, Finance officer, Bharati Vidyapeeth (Deemed to be University) Pune.

P. Madhusudan Reddy

Ex AGM, Bank of Baroda & IP

Kanchan Choudhary

ACMA and IP, Nagpur

PMV Subbarao

Practising Company Secretary and Insolvency Professional Hyderabad

K K Rao

M.Com, LL.B, FCMA, FCS, CMA, Insovency Professional, Hyderabad

Gautam Raj Choudhary

FCA, FCS & Insolvency Professional, Bangalore

P J K Reddy

M.Com., FCA, CS(I) & Insolvency Professional

Ashok Kumar Golechha

Ex General Manager UCO BANK- Insolvency Professional, Gujrat

P.Jayarama Krishna

M Com, CMA and IP, Hyderabad

PREFACE

Dear Learned Readers - Advocates, Insolvency Professionals, Chartered Accountants, Company Secretaries, Corporate Applicants, Corporate Debtors, Corporates, MNCs, IPAs, IPEs, NCLT, NCLAT, DRT & DRAT, High Courts & Supreme Court librarians, Entrepreneurs, Individuals, Consultants, Valuers, Law Students & Law School Faculties,

I am very delighted to provide you a book on *Supreme Court of India's Leading Case Laws on Insolvency & Bankruptcy Code 2016*.

In this book you will get...

1. Name of the Case i. e. Cause title
2. Relevant Sections discussed in the case
3. Hon'ble Judges/Coram of the case
4. Number of PDF Pages in Original Judgement of the case
5. All available Citations of the case
6. Case Note with appeal allowed/ dismissed or disposed off
7. Facts of the case
8. Hon'ble Apex Court's findings, while dismissing/allowing or disposing the appeal
9. Ratio Decidendi if any.

My special thanks to Manupatra, because of their web portal I can compile this book in well manner. I am also thankful to Notion Press to support me to publish and market this book throughout the

Country. Thanks to my Juniors, Advocate Colleagues and Insolvency Professional Colleagues to support me in this venture.

I hope this book will add some value addition in the wealth of your legal knowledge. Your positive feedbacks will boost me to compile/ write further books & negative feedbacks will improve my skills. Kindly send your valuable feedbacks by email.

Yours Sincerely,

Jayprakash B. Somani

Advocate, Supreme Court of India & NCLAT New Delhi

Insolvency Professional & Certified Independent Director

Email :jaysomani64@gmail.com

Web Site: www.jayprakashsomani.com

1

INNOVENTIVE INDUSTRIES LTD. VS. ICICI BANK AND ORS. (31.08.2017 – SC)

Relevant Sections: Insolvency And Bankruptcy Code, 2016 - Section 13; Section 14; Section 238; & Maharashtra Relief Undertakings (Special Provisions Act), 1958 - Section 4

Hon'ble Judges/Coram: Rohinton Fali Nariman and Sanjay Kishan Kaul, JJ.

Number of PDF Pages in Original Judgement: 49

Citations: AIR2017SC 4084, III(2017)BC 632(SC), [2017]140C LA39(SC), [2017]205C ompC as57(SC), (2017)4C ompLJ193(SC), 2017(5)CTC725, 2017(11)SCALE4, (2018)1SCC407, [2017]143SC L625(SC), (2018)1WBLR(SC)446, MANU/SC/1063/2017

Case Note: Banking - Insolvency resolution - Challenged thereto - Sections 13, 14 and 238 of Insolvency and Bankruptcy Code of 2016 and Section 4 of Maharashtra Relief Undertakings (Special Provisions Act), 1958 - Financial creditor made application, in which it was stated that the Appellant being defaulter within meaning of Code, insolvency resolution process ought to be set in motion - By order National Company Law Tribunal held that the Code would prevail against Maharashtra Act in view of non-obstante Clause in Section 238 of Code - Corporate debtor had defaulted in making payments, as per evidence placed by the financial creditors - From aforesaid order, appeal was carried to Appellate Tribunal, which met with same fate - Hence, present appeal - Whether Tribunal and Appellate Tribunal were right in admitting application filed by financial creditor.

Appeal Dismissed

Facts: Financial creditor made an application, in which it was stated that the Appellant being a defaulter within the meaning of the Code, the insolvency resolution process ought to be set in motion. It was pleaded that no default was committed by Appellant. By an order National Company Law Tribunal (NCLT) held that the Code would prevail against the Maharashtra Act in view of the non-obstante Clause in Section 238 of the Code. It, therefore, held that the Parliamentary statute would prevail over the State statute and this being so, it is obvious that the corporate debtor had defaulted in making payments, as per the evidence placed by the financial creditors. Hence, the application was admitted and a moratorium was declared. By a separate order passed by the NCLT, in which a clarification application was dismissed, it was held that the second application was raised belatedly and would not be maintainable for two reasons (i) because no audience had been given to the corporate debtor in the Tribunal by the Code; and (ii) the corporate debtor had not taken the plea contained in the second application in the earlier application. From the aforesaid order, an appeal was carried to the NCLAT, which met with the same fate. The National Company Law Appellate Tribunal (NCLAT), however, held that the Code and the Maharashtra Act operate in different fields and, therefore, were not repugnant to each other. Having recorded this, however, the NCLAT went on to hold that the Appellant cannot derive any advantage from the Maharashtra Act to stall the insolvency resolution process under Section 7 of the Code.

Hon'ble Apex Court held, while dismissing the appeal:

i. The earlier State law was repugnant to the later Parliamentary enactment as under the said State law, the State Government may take over the management of the relief undertaking, after which a temporary moratorium in much the same manner as that contained in Sections 13 and 14 of the Code takes place under Section 4 of the Maharashtra Act. There was no doubt that by giving effect to the State law, the aforesaid plan or scheme which may be adopted under the Parliamentary statute would directly be hindered and/or obstructed to that extent in that the management of the relief undertaking, which, if taken over by the State Government, would directly impede or come in the way of the taking over of the management of the corporate body by the interim resolution professional. Also, the moratorium imposed under Section 4 of the Maharashtra Act would directly clash with the moratorium to be issued under Sections 13 and 14 of the Code. It would be noticed that whereas the moratorium imposed under the Maharashtra Act was discretionary and may relate to one or more of the matters contained in Section 4(1), the moratorium imposed under the Code relates to all matters listed in Section 14 and follows as a matter of course. Unless the Maharashtra Act was out of the way, the Parliamentary enactment would be hindered and obstructed in such a manner that it would not be possible to go ahead with the insolvency resolution process outlined in the Code. Further, the non-obstante clause contained in Section 4 of the Maharashtra Act could not possibly be held to apply to the Central enactment, inasmuch as a matter of constitutional law, the later Central enactment being repugnant to the earlier State enactment, would operate to render the Maharashtra Act void vis-a-vis action taken under the later Central enactment. [55]

ii. The second application clearly appears to be an after-thought for the reason that the corporate debtor was fully aware of the fact that the Master Restructuring Agreement (MRA) had failed and could easily have pointed out these facts in the first application itself. However, for reasons best known to it, the Appellant chose to take up only a law point before the Tribunal. [57]

iii. The obligation of the corporate debtor was, therefore, unconditional and did not depend upon infusing of funds by the creditors into the Appellant company. Also, the argument taken for the first time before present Court that no debt was in fact due under the MRA as it has not fallen due (owing to the default of the secured creditor) was not something that could be countenanced at this stage of the proceedings. The Tribunal and the Appellate Tribunal were right in admitting the application filed by the financial creditor. [59]

Legal Latin Terms Group 1

a fortiori - With stronger reason

a priori - From the cause to the effect

ab initio - From the beginning

actiones in personam - Personal actions

ad curiam - Before a court; to court

ad damnum clause - To the damage, clause in a complaint stating monetary loss

ad faciendum - To do

ad hoc - For this purpose or occasion

ad litem - For this suit or litigation

ad rem - To the thing at hand

ad valorem - According to the value

2

SURENDRA TRADING COMPANY VS. JUGGILAL KAMLAPAT JUTE MILLS COMPANY LTD. AND ORS. (19.09.2017 – SC)

Relevant Section: Sections 7(5), 9(5) and 10(4) of Insolvency and Bankruptcy Code, 2016

Hon'ble Judges/Coram: A.K. Sikri and Ashok Bhushan, JJ.

Number of PDF Pages in Original Judgement: 16

Citations: 2018(2)ABR324, AIR2018SC186, 2018(1)AKR 663, 2018(4)ALLMR462, [2017]141CLA174(SC), [2017]205CompCas119(SC), (2018)1CompLJ217(SC), 2018-1-LW813, (2017)16SCC143, 2019 (1) SCJ 641, [2017]144SCL198(SC), MANU/SC/1248/2017

Case Note: Company - Removal of defects - Expiry of time - Sections 7(5), 9(5) and 10(4) of Insolvency and Bankruptcy Code, 2016 - National Company Law Appellate Tribunal held that time of seven days prescribed in proviso to Sub-section (5) of Section 9 of Code was mandatory in nature and if defects contained in application filed by operational creditor for initiating corporate insolvency resolution against corporate debtor were not removed within seven days of receipt of notice given by adjudicating authority for removal of such objections, then such application filed under Section 9 of Code was liable to be rejected - Hence, present appeal - Whether provision of removing defects within seven days was mandatory in nature.

Appeal Allowed.

Facts: The National Company Law Appellate Tribunal was held that the time of seven days prescribed in proviso to Sub-section (5) of Section 9 of the Insolvency and Bankruptcy Code, 2016 was mandatory in nature and if the defects contained in the application filed by the operational creditor for initiating corporate insolvency resolution against a corporate debtor were not removed within seven days of the receipt of notice given by the adjudicating authority for removal of such objections, then such an application filed under Section 9 of the Code was liable to be rejected.

Hon'ble Apex Court held, while allowing the appeal:

i. This Court was not able to decipher any valid reason given while coming to the conclusion that the period mentioned in proviso was mandatory. The order of the NCLAT, proceeds to take note of the provisions of Section 12 of the Code and points out the time limit for completion of insolvency resolution process was one hundred eighty days, which period could be extended by another ninety days However, that could hardly provide any justification to construe the provisions of proviso to Sub-section (5) of Section 9 in the manner in which it was done. It was to be borne in mind that limit of one hundred eighty days mentioned in Section 12 also starts from the date of admission of the application. Period prior thereto which was consumed, after the filing of the application under Section 9, whether by the Registry of the adjudicating authority in scrutinising the application or by the applicant in removing the defects or by the adjudicating authority in admitting the application is not to be taken into account. In fact, till the objections were removed it is not to be treated as application validly filed inasmuch as only after the application was complete in every respect it was required to be entertained. In this scenario, making the period of seven days contained in the proviso as mandatory did not commend to this Court. No purpose was going to be served by treating this period as mandatory. In a given case there may be weighty, valid and justifiable reasons for not able to remove the defects within seven days. Notwithstanding the same, the effect would be to reject the application. [20]

ii. The moot question would be as to whether such a rejection would be treated as rejecting the application on merits thereby debarring the application from filing fresh application or it is to be treated as an administrative order since the rejection was because of the reason that defects were not removed and application was not examined on merits. In the former case it would be travesty of justice that even if the case of the applicant on merits is very strong, the applicant was shown the door without adjudication of his application on merits. If the latter alternative was accepted, then rejection of the application in the first instance was not going to serve any purpose as the applicant would be permitted to file fresh application, complete in all aspects, which would have to be entertained. Thus, in either case, no purpose was served by treating the said provision as mandatory. [21]

iii. The judgments cited by the NCLAT and the principle contained therein applied while deciding that period of fourteen days within which the adjudicating authority had to pass the order is not mandatory but directory in nature would equally apply while interpreting proviso to Sub-section (5) of Section 7, Section 9 or Sub-section (4) of Section 10 as well. After all, the applicant did not gain anything by not removing the objections inasmuch as till the objections were removed, such an application would not be entertained. Therefore, it was in the interest of the applicant to remove the defects as early as possible. [23]

iv. Therefore, part of the impugned judgment of NCLAT which holds proviso to Sub-section (5) of Section 7 or proviso to Sub-section (5) of Section 9 or proviso to Sub-section (4) of Section 10 to remove the defects within seven days as mandatory and on failure applications to be rejected, was set aside. [26]

Legal Latin Terms Group 2

adversus - Against

aggregatio menium - Contractual meeting of the minds

alias dictus - An assumed name

alibi - In another place, elsewhere

aliunde - From another place, from without (as in evidence outside the document)

alter ego - The other self

amicus curiae - "friend of the court" brief

animo - With intention, disposition, design or will

animus - Mind or intention

ante litem motam - before the suit or before litigation is filed

arguendo - In the course of an argument

3

MOBILOX INNOVATIONS PRIVATE LIMITED VS. KIRUSA SOFTWARE PRIVATE LIMITED (21.09.2017 – SC)

Relevant Section: Sections 8 and 9 of Insolvency and Bankruptcy Code, 2016 & Legislative Guide on Insolvency Law of the United Nations Commission on International Trade Law

Hon'ble Judges/Coram: Rohinton Fali Nariman and Sanjay Kishan Kaul, JJ.

Number of PDF Pages in Original Judgement: 45

Citation: AIR2017SC4532, 2017 6 AWC5658SC, IV(2017) BC445(SC), [2017]140CLA123(SC), [2017]205CompCas324(SC), (2017)4CompLJ255(SC), 2017(5)CTC831, 2018(1)RCR(Civil)725, 2017(11)SCALE754, (2018)1SCC353, 2017 (9) SCJ 300, [2017]144SCL37(SC), MANU/SC/1196/2017

Case Note: Insolvency - Operational debt - Liability thereof - Sections 8 and 9 of Insolvency and Bankruptcy Code, 2016 - Application was filed before National Company Law Tribunal under Sections 8 and 9 of new Code stating that operational debt was owed to Respondent - Tribunal dismissed application - Appeal was then filed before National Company Law Appellate Tribunal which was allowed - Hence, present appeal - Whether there was existence of dispute between parties or record of pendency of suit filed before receipt of demand notice of unpaid operational debt in relation to such dispute.

Appeal Allowed

Facts: An application was then filed before the National Company Law Tribunal under Sections 8 and 9 of the new Code stating that an operational debt was owed to the Respondent. The Tribunal dismissed the aforesaid application. An appeal was then filed before the National Company Law Appellate Tribunal which was allowed. Hence, present appeal.

Hon'ble Apex Court held, while allowing the appeal:

Once the operational creditor has filed an application, which was otherwise complete, the Adjudicating Authority must reject the application under Section 9(5)(2)(d) if notice of dispute has been received by the operational creditor or there was a record of dispute in the information utility. It was clear that such notice must bring to the notice of the operational creditor the existence of a dispute or the fact that a suit or arbitration proceeding relating to a dispute was pending between the parties. Therefore, all that the adjudicating Authority was to see at this stage was whether there was a plausible contention which requires further investigation and that the dispute was not a patently feeble legal argument or an assertion of fact unsupported by evidence. It was important to separate the grain from the chaff and to reject a spurious defence which was mere bluster. However, in doing so, the Court did not need to be satisfied that the defence was likely to succeed. The Court did not at this stage examine the merits of the dispute. So long as a dispute truly exists in fact and was not spurious, hypothetical or illusory, the Adjudicating Authority has to reject the application. The confirmation from a financial institution that there was no payment of an unpaid operational debt by the corporate debtor was an important piece of information that needs to be placed before the Adjudicating Authority, under Section 9 of the Code, but given the fact that the Adjudicating Authority had not dismissed the application on this ground and that the Appellant had raised this ground only at the Appellate stage, the application could not be dismissed at the threshold for want of this certificate alone. [40] and [41]

Legal Latin Terms Group 3

assumpsit - He undertook or promised

bona fide - Good faith

capias - Take, arrest

captia - Persons, or heads

causa mortis - By reason of death

caveat - Beware, a warning

caveat emptor - "Let the buyer beware"

certiorari - "send the pleadings up", indicating a discretionary review process

Cestui - Beneficiaries

Cestui que trust - Beneficiaries of a trust

4

MACQUARIE BANK LIMITED VS. SHILPI CABLE TECHNOLOGIES LTD. (15.12.2017 – SC)

Relevant Section: Section 9(3)(c) of Insolvency and Bankruptcy Code, 2016

Hon'ble Judges/Coram: Rohinton Fali Nariman and Navin Sinha, JJ.

Number of PDF Pages in Original Judgement: 33

Citation: AIR2018SC498, 2018(3)ALD87, 2018 2 AWC1277SC, I(2018)BC219(SC), 2018(2)BomCR212, [2018]142CLA1(SC), (2018)1CompLJ270(SC), (2018)2MLJ552, 2018(1)RCR(Civil)472, 2017(14)SCALE509, (2018)2SCC674, 2018 (1) SCJ 646, [2018]145SCL236(SC), MANU/SC/1609/2017

Case Note: Insolvency - Operational Debt - Valuation thereof - Section 9(3)(c) of Insolvency and Bankruptcy Code, 2016 (Code) - Present appeal against order of National Company Law Appellate Tribunal (NCLAT) whereby Appellants application dismissed for non-compliance of mandatory provision of Section 9(3)(c) of Code - Whether, in relation to operational debt, provision contained in Section 9(3)(c) of Code mandatory - Whether demand notice of unpaid operational debt be issued by lawyer on behalf of operational creditor –

Appeal Allowed

Facts: An agreement was executed by which the Appellant purchase the supplier's right, title and interest in favor of the Respondent. Based on the agreement, a sales contract was made between the parties. Subsequently, the Appellant issued two invoices and demanded for payment due. After the enactment of the Code, a demand notice under Section of the Code was issued to the Respondent to pay the outstanding amount. The Appellant initiated the insolvency proceedings by filing a petition Under Section 9 of the Code. The NCLAT agreed with the National Company Law Tribunal (NCLT) holding that the application would have to be dismissed for non compliance of the mandatory provision contained in Section 9(3)(c) of the Code. Hence, present appeal preferred.

Hon'ble Apex Court held, while allowing the appeal:

i. There may be situations of operational creditors who may have dealings with a financial institution as defined in Section 3(14) of the Code. There may also be situations where an operational creditor may have as his banker a non-scheduled bank, for example, in which case, it would be impossible for him to fulfill the aforesaid condition. A foreign supplier or assignee of such supplier may have a foreign banker who is not within Section 3(14) of the Code. The fact that such foreign supplier is an operational creditor is established from a reading of the definition of "person" contained in Section 3(23), as including persons resident outside India, together with the definition of "operational creditor" contained in Section 5(20), which in turn is defined as "a person to whom an operational debt is owed and includes any person to whom such debt has been legally assigned or transferred". That such person may have a bank/financial institution with whom it deals and which is not contained within the definition of Section 3(14) of the Code would show that Section 9(3)(c) in such a case would, if the Sub-section being a condition precedent, amount to a threshold bar to proceeding further under the Code. The Code cannot be construed in a discriminatory fashion so as to include only those operational creditors who are residents outside India who happen to bank with financial institutions which may be included Under Section 3(14) of the Code. It is no answer to state that such person can approach the Central Government to include its foreign banker Under Section 3(14) of the Code, for the Central Government may never do so. Such persons ought to be left out of the triggering of the Code against their corporate debtor, despite being operational creditors as defined, would not sound well with Article 14 of the Constitution, which applies to all persons including foreigners. Therefore, as the facts of these cases show, a so called condition precedent impossible of compliance cannot be put as a threshold bar to the processing of an application Under Section of the Code. [14]

ii. It is true that the expression "initiation" contained in the marginal note to Section does indicate the drift of the provision, but from such drift, to build an argument that the expression "initiation" would lead to the conclusion that Section 9(3) contains mandatory conditions precedent before which the Code can be triggered is a long shot. Equally, the expression "shall" in Section 9(3) does not take us much further when it is clear that Section 9(3)(c) becomes impossible of compliance in cases like the present. It would amount to a situation where in serious general inconvenience would be caused to innocent persons, such as the Appellant, without very much furthering the object of the Act. [19]

5

BANK OF NEW YORK MELLON, LONDON BRANCH VS. ZENITH INFOTECH LIMITED (21.02.2017 – SC)

Relevant Section: Section 3(e), 3(f) and Section 15 of the SICA & Section 252 of Insolvency and Bankruptcy Code, 2016

Hon'ble Judges/Coram: Ranjan Gogoi and Abhay Manohar Sapre, JJ.

Number of PDF Pages in Original Judgement: 14

Citation: AIR2017SC1735, 2017 (124) ALR 525, [2017]137CLA71(SC), [2017]201CompCas280(SC), (2017)2CompLJ6(SC), 2017-5-LW105, 2017(5)MhLj269, (2017)3MLJ614, 2017(4)MPLJ252, 2017(3)SCALE98, (2017)5SCC1, 2017 (4) SCJ 61, [2017]140SCL333(SC), MANU/SC/0191/2017

Case Note: SICA - Application for reference - Registration thereof - Power and jurisdiction - Winding up order - Impact thereof - Sick Industrial Companies (Special Provisions) Act, 1985 (SICA) - Orders of Secretary and Chairman of Board rejecting Respondent No. 1's application for Reference were subjected to challenge before High Court - High Court held that Registrar and other authorities like Secretary and Chairman of Board had not been conferred any power of adjudication - Further, winding up order passed by

Company Court would not foreclose proceedings under SICA - Registration of Reference and inquiry can still be made - Hence, present appeal - Whether power and jurisdiction of Registrar and Secretary to refuse registration of application for reference made by Respondent company were sustainable-

Disposed off

Facts: The Respondent No. 1 company filed a Reference before the Board Under Section 15 of the Sick Industrial Companies (Special Provisions) Act, 1985 (SICA). The said application was refused registration by the Registrar of the Board on the ground that Respondent No. 1 company was not an industrial company within the meaning of Section 3(e) and 3(f) of the SICA. An appeal was filed by the Respondent No. 1 company before the Secretary of the Board against the order of Registrar which was dismissed. There was a further appeal to the Chairman of the Board against the order of the Secretary. The Chairman of the Board also dismissed the second appeal filed by the Respondent No. 1 company by order.

A petition for winding up of the Respondent No. 1 company was admitted by the High Court and the order of admission was affirmed by the Division Bench in appeal. The approach to the present Court also was not successful. Thereafter, the High Court passed orders for winding up of the Respondent No. 1 which was upheld in appeal by the Division Bench of the High Court. Though, a stay was ordered by the High Court of its winding up order till 31.08.2014, it would appear that the High Court understood the said interim order to have been vacated by efflux of time, in the absence of any specific order of extension. Thereafter the Official Liquidator came to be appointed by the High Court on 02.09.2014.

The orders of the Secretary and Chairman of the Board rejecting the application for Reference filed by the Respondent No. 1 company were subjected to a challenge in a writ petition filed by the Respondent-company before the High Court out of which the present proceedings were arisen. Two questions arose before the High Court of Delhi in the writ petition. The first was whether the dismissal of the application for Reference by the Registrar, Secretary and Chairman of the Board was within the jurisdiction of the said authorities. The second question, which was implicit if there was to be a positive answer to the first, was whether in view of the order of winding up passed by the Company Court, and affirmed by the Division Bench of the High Court, there is any further scope for registration of the Reference sought for by the Respondent No. 1 company under the provisions of the SICA if the order declining registration by the aforesaid authorities is to be understood to be non est.

The High Court took the view that under the provisions of the SICA read with the Regulations, the Registrar and the other authorities like the Secretary and the Chairman of the Board have not been conferred any power of adjudication which would necessarily be involved in determining the question as to whether the Respondent No. 1 company was an industrial company within the meaning of Section 3(e) and 3(f) of the SICA. Since an adjudicatory function and role had been performed by the Registrar, whose order had been affirmed by the Secretary and the Chairman of the Board and as registration of the Reference sought for by the Respondent No. 1 company was refused on that basis the said orders were non est in law. Regarding the second question, the High Court relying on the decisions of the present Court in Real Value Appliances Ltd. v. Canara Bank and Ors. and Rishabh Agro Industries Ltd. v. P.N.B. Capital Services Ltd. concluded that the winding up order passed by the Company Court would not foreclose the proceedings under the SICA and registration of a Reference Under Section 15 and the inquiry Under Section 16 can still be made. The question that was agitated in the present appeal was consequential to the above determination and revolve around the application of Section 22 of SICA to bar further steps in the winding up proceeding before the High Court. The above question would no longer survive in the context of the provisions of the now repealed Act but would still require an answer from the stand point of the provisions of the Insolvency and Bankruptcy Code in force with effect from 1.12.2016.

Hon'ble Apex Court held, while disposing off the appeal:

i. On receipt of a Reference under Regulation 19(4) of the Board for Industrial and Financial Reconstruction Regulations, 1987 the Secretary or the Registrar, as may be, after making an endorsement of the date on which the same has been received in the office of the Board is required to make a scrutiny and, thereafter, if found to be in order, to register the same; assign a serial number thereto and place the same before the Chairman for being assigned to a Bench. After completion of the aforesaid exercise under Regulation 19(5) the later part of the said Regulation contemplates that simultaneously, remaining information/documents required, if any, may be called for from the applicant. Regulation 20 contained in Chapter III and Regulation 21 contained in Chapter IV deal with the manner in which the proceedings of inquiry after registration of the Reference is to be made. Regulation 19(5) requires the Registrar or the Secretary, as may be, to make an endorsement of the date of receipt of the Reference [Regulation 19(4)] and thereafter on scrutiny thereof to register the same and place before the Chairman for being referred to the Bench. When the Regulations framed under the statute vests in the Registrar or the Secretary of the Board the power to "scrutinize" an application prior to registration thereof and thereafter to register and place the same before the Bench, no reason to see how such power of scrutiny can be understood to be vesting in any of the said authorities the power to adjudicate the question as to whether a company is an industrial company within the meaning of Section 3(e) read with 3(f) and 3(n) of the SICA. A claim to come within the ambit of the aforesaid provisions of the SICA i.e. to be an industrial company, more often than not, would be a contentious issue. In the present case, it certainly was. The specific stand of the Respondent No. 1 company in this regard need not detain the Court save and except to state that by a detailed description of the manufacturing process the Respondent No. 1 company had sought to contend that it was an industrial company. Surely, the rejection of the above stand could have been made only by a process of adjudication which power and jurisdiction clearly and undoubtedly was vested by the SICA and the Regulations framed thereunder in a Bench of the Board and not in authorities like the Registrar and the Secretary. The High Court was correct in coming to the conclusion that the refusal of registration of the reference sought by the Respondent Company by the Registrar, Secretary/Chairman of the Board was non-est in law. The reference must, therefore, understood to be pending before the Board on the relevant date attracting the provisions of Section 252 of the Insolvency and Bankruptcy Code. [16],[17] and[18]

ii. The second question was answered in the negative relying on Real Value Appliances Ltd. v. Canara Bank and Ors. and Rishabh Agro Industries Ltd. v. P.N.B. Capital Services Ltd. The core principles laid down in the said decisions of the Court, namely, that immediately on registration of a reference Under Section 15 of the erstwhile SICA, the enquiry Under Section 16 is deemed to have commenced and that the winding up proceedings against a company stood terminated only after orders Under Section 481 of the Companies Act, 1956, were passed, will have to be noticed to adjudge the correctness of the said view of the High Court. In any event, the aforesaid question becomes redundant in view of the conclusion that the reference sought by the Respondent Company must be deemed to have been pending on the date of commencement of the Insolvency and Bankruptcy Code, particularly, Section 252 thereof. It would still be open to the Respondent to seek its remedies under the provisions of Section 252 of the Code read with what is laid down in Sections 13, 14, 20 and 25. [19] and[20]

6

ANUJ JAIN VS. AXIS BANK LIMITED AND ORS. (26.02.2020 – SC)

Relevant Section: Sections 3(10), 5, 5(7), 5(8), 43, 43(4), 44, 45 and 66 of Insolvency and Bankruptcy Code, 2016

Hon'ble Judges/Coram: Ranjan Gogoi and Abhay Manohar Sapre, JJ.

Number of PDF Pages in Original Judgement: 95

Citation : MANU/SC/0228/2020, [2020]155CLA139(SC)

Case Note: Company - Preferential transactions - Financial creditor - Sections 3(10), 5, 5(7), 5(8), 43, 43(4), 44, 45 and 66 of Insolvency and Bankruptcy Code, 2016 - Interim Resolution Professional moved application in Corporate Insolvency Resolution Process concerning Corporate Debtor Company seeking avoidance of certain transactions, whereby corporate debtor had mortgaged its properties as collateral securities for loans and advances made by lender banks and financial institutions to holding company, as being preferential, undervalued and fraudulent, in terms of Sections 43, 45 and 66 of Code - Company Law Tribunal held that transactions in question were to defraud lenders of corporate debtor - Tribunal declared impugned transactions as fraudulent, preferential and undervalued transactions - Assailing said order passed by Tribunal accepting application of IRP in relation to six of mortgage transactions, aggrieved parties filed appeals before Appellate Tribunal - Appellate Tribunal set aside impugned order passed by Tribunal - Hence, present appeal - Whether transactions in question deserve to be avoided as being preferential, undervalued and fraudulent, in terms of Sections 43, 45 and 66 of Code and Respondents could be recognized as financial creditors of corporate debtor. –

Appeal Allowed.

Facts: An application moved by the Interim Resolution Professional in the Corporate Insolvency Resolution Process concerning the Corporate Debtor Company seeking avoidance of certain transactions, whereby the corporate debtor had mortgaged its properties as collateral securities for the loans and advances made by the lender banks and financial institutions to the holding company of corporate debtor company, as being preferential, undervalued and fraudulent, in terms of Sections 43, 45 and 66 of the Insolvency and Bankruptcy Code, 2016. The National Company Law Tribunal after having heard the parties and having scanned through the record, held that the transactions in question were to defraud the lenders of the corporate debtor. The company application filed by the Resolution Professional under Section 66, 43 and 45 of the Insolvency and Bankruptcy 2016 was allowed. The impugned transactions, details of which were given in the Schedule of the judgment were declared as fraudulent, preferential and undervalued transactions as defined under Section 66, 43 and 45 of the Code respectively. Assailing the aforesaid order passed by NCLT accepting the application of IRP in relation to six of the mortgage transactions, the aggrieved parties filed separate appeals before the Appellate Tribunal, the NCLAT. The Appellate Tribunal took note of the facts of the case and the rival contentions and proceeded to upturn the order passed by NCLT.

Hon'ble Apex Court held, while allowing the appeals:

i. The transactions in question had been of deemed preference to related party by the corporate debtor during the look-back period of two years and have rightly been held covered within the period envisaged by Sub-section (4) of Section 43 of the Code. [24.5]

ii. Taking up the transactions in question, this court was of the view that even when furnishing a security may be one of normal business practices, it would become a part of ordinary course of business of a particular corporate entity only if it falls in place as part of the undistinguished common flow of business done and was not arising out of any special or particular situation, as rightly expressed in Downs Distributing Co.. Though this court may assume that the transactions in question were entered in the ordinary course of business of bankers and financial institutions like the present Respondents but on the given set of facts, we have not an iota of doubt that the impugned transactions did not fall within the ordinary course of business of the corporate debtor. The corporate debtor had been promoted as a special purpose vehicle by holding company for construction and operation of Yamuna Expressway and for development of the parcels of land along with the expressway for residential, commercial and other use. It was difficult to even surmise that the business of corporate debtor company, of ensuring execution of the works assigned to its holding company and for execution of housing/building projects, in its ordinary course, had inflated itself to the extent of routinely mortgaging its assets and/or inventories to secure the debts of its holding company. It had also not been the ordinary course of financial affairs of corporate debtor company that it would create encumbrances over its properties to secure the debts of its holding company. In other words, the ordinary course of business or financial affairs of the corporate debtor could not be taken to be that of providing mortgages to secure the loans and facilities obtained by its holding company and that too at the cost of its own financial health. As noticed, corporate debtor company was already reeling under debts with its accounts with some of the lenders having been declared NPA and it was also under heavy pressure to honour its commitment to the home buyers. In the given circumstances, the transfers in questions were not made in ordinary course of business or financial affairs of the corporate debtor. [25.6.2]

iii. The transactions in question were hit by Section 43 of the Code and the Adjudicating Authority, having rightly held so, had been justified in issuing necessary directions in terms of Section 44 of the Code in relation to the transactions concerning Property. Appellate Tribunal had not been right in interfering with the well-considered and justified order passed by Tribunal. [27]

iv. A person having only security interest over the assets of corporate debtor (like the instant third party securities), even if falling within the description of secured creditor by virtue of collateral security extended by the corporate debtor, would nevertheless stand outside the sect of financial creditors' as per the definitions contained in Sub-sections (7) and (8) of Section 5 of the Code. Differently put, if a corporate debtor has given its property in mortgage to secure the debts of a third party, it may lead to a mortgage debt and, therefore, it may fall within the definition of debt under Section 3(10) of the Code. However, it would remain a debt alone and could not partake the character of a financial debt within the meaning of Section 5(8) of the Code. [47.2]

v. Such lenders of holding company, on the strength of the mortgages in question, may fall in the category of secured creditors, but such mortgages being neither towards any loan, facility or advance to the corporate debtor nor towards protecting any facility or security of the corporate debtor, it could not be said that the corporate debtor owes them any financial debt within the meaning of Section 5 of the Code and hence, such lenders of holding company did not fall in the category of the 'financial creditors' of the corporate debtor. [54]

7

ARCELORMITTAL INDIA PRIVATE LIMITED VS. SATISH KUMAR GUPTA AND ORS. (04.10.2018 – SC)

Relevant Section: Section 29A of Insolvency and Bankruptcy Code, 2016

Hon'ble Judges/Coram: Rohinton Fali Nariman and Indu Malhotra, JJ.

Number of PDF Pages in Original Judgement: 81

Citation: AIR2018SC5646, IV(2018)BC380(SC), [2018]146CLA293(SC), [2018]211CompCas369(SC), (2018)4CompLJ141(SC), 2019(1)CTC291, 2018(13)SCALE381, (2019)2SCC1, 2019 (4) SCJ 139, [2018]150SCL354(SC), MANU/SC/1123/2018

Case Note: Company - Resolution plan - Ineligibility thereof - Section 29A of Insolvency and Bankruptcy Code, 2016 - Adjudicating Authority, admitting petition filed for financial debts owed to creditors by corporate debtor and appointed Interim Resolution Professional - Resolution Professional published advertisement, for submit resolution plans for revival of company - Appellant and one other company submitted their resolution plans - Resolution Professional found both companies to be ineligible under Section 29A of Code - Application was filed before Company Tribunal against said order which was dismissed - Appeals were filed before Appellate Tribunal, Tribunal confirmed order of ineligibility of resolution applicants to submit resolution plans - Hence, present appeal - Whether Appellant-resolution applicant was eligible to submit resolution plan.

Disposed off

Facts: Adjudicating Authority, passed an order under Section 7 the Insolvency and Bankruptcy Code, 2016 at the behest of financial creditors, admitting a petition filed under the Code for financial debts owed to them by the corporate debtor and appointed the Interim Resolution Professional. Resolution Professional published advertisement, seeking expression of interest from potential resolution applicants who wished to submit resolution plans for the revival of company. Appellant and one company submitted their resolution plans. Resolution Professional found both companies to be ineligible under Section 29A of Code. On appeal, the Company Tribunal found that there was no patent illegality in the decision of the RP for declaring ineligible to applicants. Appeals were filed by both companies against said order which was dismissed.

Hon'ble Apex Court held, while disposing off the appeal:

i. The interpretation of Section 29A(c) of Code becomes clear. Any person who wishes to submit a resolution plan, if he or it does so acting jointly, or in concert with other persons, which person or other persons happen to either manage or control or be promoters of a corporate debtor, who is classified as a non-performing asset and whose debts have not been paid off for a period of at least one year before commencement of the corporate insolvency resolution process, becomes ineligible to submit a resolution plan. This provision therefore ensures that if a person wishes to submit a resolution plan, and if such person or any person acting jointly or any person in concert with such person, happens to either manage, control, or be promoter of a corporate debtor declared as a non-performing asset one year before the corporate insolvency resolution process begins, is ineligible to submit a resolution plan. The first proviso to Sub-clause (c) makes it clear that the ineligibility can only be removed if the person submitting a resolution plan makes payment of all overdue amounts with interest thereon and charges relating to the non-performing asset in question before submission of a resolution plan. The position in law is thus clear. Any person who wishes to submit a resolution plan acting jointly or in concert with other persons, any of whom may either manage, control or be a promoter of a corporate debtor classified as a non-performing asset in the period abovementioned, must first pay off the debt of the said corporate debtor classified as a non-performing asset in order to become eligible under Section 29A(c) of Act. [54]

ii. The time limit for completion of the insolvency resolution process is laid down in Section 12 of Code. A period of one hundred eighty days from the date of admission of the application is given by Section 12(1) of Code. This is extendable by a maximum period of ninety days only if the Committee of Creditors, by a vote to extend the said period, and only if the Adjudicating Authority is satisfied that such process cannot be completed within one hundred eighty days. The authority may then, by order, extend the duration of such process by a maximum period of ninety days. What was also of importance was the proviso to Section 12(3) of Code which states that any extension of the period under Section 12 of Code could nnot be granted more than once. This had to be read with the third proviso to Section 30(4) of Code, which states that the maximum period of thirty days mentioned in the second proviso is allowable as the only exception to the extension of the said period not being granted more than once. [70]

iii. The importance of the Resolution Professional is to ensure that a resolution plan was complete in all respects, and to conduct a due diligence in order to report to the Committee of Creditors whether or not it was in order. Even though it was not necessary for the Resolution Professional to give reasons while submitting a resolution plan to the Committee of Creditors, it would be in the fitness of things if he appends the due diligence report carried out by him with respect to each of the resolution plans under consideration, and to state briefly as to why it does or does not conform to the law. [78]

iv. A few days before Appellant submitted its first resolution plan, parent company sold its entire shareholding in promoter company by way of an off market sale, to a company of the Indian co-promoters. The sale of shares was done without making an open offer under the 2011 Takeover Regulations, on the basis that it was an inter se transfer of shares between promoters, and therefore exempt from such requirement Under Regulation 10 of the said Regulations. Also, as a matter of fact, the sale of the said shares was effected without taking the consent of the lenders of Uttam Galva, which consent was necessary as per the Non Disclosure Undertaking that was executed by parent company. Consequent to the said inter se transfer, the Co-Promotion Agreement was said to have stood automatically terminated. By way of abundant caution, a formal deed of termination was entered into. [108]

v. It was absolutely clear that a person, who was the ultimate shareholder of the resolution applicant was directly the ultimate shareholder of parent company. When the corporate veil of the various companies mentioned was pierced, both Applicant and parent company were found to be managed and controlled by said person and were therefore persons deemed to be acting in concert as per Regulation 2(1)(q)(2)(i) of the 2011 Takeover Regulations. That parent company was a promoter of company was clear from the aforementioned facts, being expressly stated as such in promoter company 's annual returns. The reasonably proximate facts prior to the submission of both resolution plans by resolution applicant would show that there was no doubt whatsoever that parent company's shares in promoter company were sold only in order to get out of the ineligibility mentioned by Section 29A(c) of Act, and consequently the proviso thereto. The fact that the lenders with whom parent company had a Non Disposal Undertaking have not yet moved any forum for a declaration that the sale of the shares, being without their consent, was non est, did not absolve parent company from having failed to first obtain their consent before selling off its shares in promoter company. Such sale was directly contrary to the Non Disposal Undertaking given to the lenders. Quite apart from this, it was also clear that shares were sold at a distress value, so as to overcome the provisions of Section 29A(c) of Act and the proviso thereto. It is clear therefore that the Uttam Galva transaction clearly renders Appellant-resolution applicant ineligible under Section 29A(c) of the Code. [109]

Legal Latin Terms Group 4

circa - In the area of, about or concerning

compos mentis - Of sound mind

consortium - The conjugal fellowship of husband and wife

contra - Against

coram nobis - Before us ourselves

corpus - Body

corpus delicti - Body of the offense

cum testamento annexo - "With the will annexed"

datum - Information or the thing given

de facto - In fact, in deed or actually

de jure - Of right, lawful

8

VIJAY KUMAR JAIN VS. STANDARD CHARTERED BANK AND ORS. (31.01.2019 – SC)

Relevant Section: Section 5, Section 21, Section 24, Section 25, Section 29, Section 30 & Section 31 of Insolvency and Bankruptcy Code, 2016

Hon'ble Judges/Coram: Rohinton Fali Nariman and Navin Sinha, JJ.

Number of PDF Pages in Original Judgement: 25

Citation: AIR2019SC2477, I(2019)BC482(SC), [2019]148CLA542(SC), 123(1)CWN347, 2019(1)RCR(Civil)865, 2019(2)SCALE352, 2019 (8) SCJ 658, [2019]152SCL56(SC), MANU/SC/0111/2019

Case Note: Company - Resolution plans - Committee of creditors - Right to participate - Meetings - Sections 21, 25, 30 of Insolvency and Bankruptcy Code, 2016; Regulations 25, 34, 38 of Insolvency and Bankruptcy Board of India (Insolvency Resolution Process for Corporate Persons) Regulations, 2016 [CIRP Regulations] - Present appeal arose out of an Appellate Tribunal's judgment rejecting Appellant's prayer for directions to resolution professional to provide all relevant documents including insolvency resolution plans in question to members of suspended Board of Directors of corporate debtor in each case so that, they might meaningfully participate in meetings held by committee of creditors [CoC] - Whether Appellate Tribunal which recognized Appellant's right to attend and participate in CoC meetings, but denied Appellant's prayer to access certain documents, most particularly, resolution plans was sustainable.

Appeal Allowed

Facts: Ruchi Soya Industries Ltd.- corporate debtor, was incorporated on 6th January, 1986. It was said to be a profit-making company in business of processing of oil-seeds and refining crude oil for edible use. In September, 2017, Company Petition were filed by Standard Chartered Bank Ltd. and DBS Bank Ltd., being financial creditors of aforesaid corporate debtor. These two company petitions were admitted on 8th and 15th December, 2017, respectively, by National Company Law Tribunal [NCLT]. One Shri Shailendra Ajmera of Ernst and Young was appointed as Interim Resolution Professional in both petitions. CoC was constituted under Section 21 of Insolvency and Bankruptcy Code, 2016 [Insolvency Code], and Appellant being a member of suspended Board of Directors was given notice and agenda for first CoC meeting held on 12th January, 2018, and was permitted to attend aforesaid meeting. He alleged, which was disputed by Respondents, that subsequent meetings of CoC were held in which he was denied participation. Appellant filed Miscellaneous Application before NCLT in order that, Appellant be allowed to effectively participate in these meetings. In tenth meeting dated 12th August, 2018, Appellant executed a nondisclosure agreement for sharing resolution plans of corporate debtor. Under said agreement, Appellant undertook to indemnify resolution professional and keep information that was received as to resolution plan strictly confidential. NCLT dismissed application with liberty to Appellant to attend CoC meetings but not to insist upon being provided information considered confidential either by resolution professional or committee of creditors. Against this order, Appellant filed an appeal before Appellate Tribunal which recognized Appellant's right to attend and participate in CoC meetings, but denied Appellant's prayer to access certain documents, most particularly, resolution plans. Thereafter, an application for modification/clarification of Appellate Tribunal's order was also dismissed. Aggrieved by order of Appellate Tribunal, Appellants had filed present appeal.

Hon'ble Apex Court held, while allowing the appeal

1. Statutory scheme of Insolvency and Bankruptcy Code, 2016 made it clear that though erstwhile Board of Directors were not members of committee of creditors, yet, they had a right to participate in each and every meeting held by committee of creditors, and also had a right to discuss along with members of committee of creditors all resolution plans that were presented at such meetings under Section 25(2)(i). Operational creditors, who might participate in such meetings but had no right to vote, were vitally interested in such resolution plans, and must be furnished copies of such plans beforehand if they were to participate effectively in meeting of committee of creditors. Under Section 30(2)(b), repayment of their debts was an important part of resolution plan qua them on which they must comment. Even though persons such as operational creditors had no right to vote but were only participants in meetings of committee of creditors, yet, they would certainly had a right to be given a copy of resolution plans before such meetings were held so that they might effectively comment on same to safeguard their interest. [9]

2. Every participant was entitled to a notice of every meeting of committee of creditors. Such notice of meeting must contain an agenda of meeting, together with copies of all documents relevant for matters to be discussed and issues to be voted upon at meeting vide Regulation 21(3)(iii). Obviously, resolution plans were "matters to be discussed" at such meetings, and erstwhile Board of Directors were "participants" who would discuss these issues. Expression "documents" was a wide expression which would certainly include resolution plans. [13]

3. Under Regulation 24(2)(e), resolution professional had to take a roll call of every participant attending through video conferencing or other audio and visual means, and must state for record that such person had received agenda and all relevant material for meeting which would include resolution plan to be discussed at such meeting. Regulation 35 made it clear that, resolution professional shall provide fair value and liquidation value to every member of the committee only after receipt of resolution plans in accordance with Code. Also, under Regulation 38(1)(a), a resolution plan shall include a statement as to how it had dealt with interest of all stakeholders, and under Sub-clause 3(a), a resolution plan shall demonstrate that, it addressed cause of default. This Regulation also, therefore, recognized vital interest of erstwhile Board of Directors in a resolution plan together with cause of default. Erstwhile directors could represent to committee of creditors that, cause of default was not due to erstwhile management, but due to other factors which might be beyond their control, which had led to non-payment of debt. Therefore, a combined reading of Code as well as Regulations led to conclusion that, members of erstwhile Board of Directors, being vitally interested in resolution plans that might be discussed at meetings of committee of creditors, must be given a copy of such plans as part of "documents" that had to be furnished along with notice of such meetings. [14]

4. Regarding confidential information was concerned, it was clear that, resolution professional could take an undertaking from members of erstwhile Board of Directors, as had been taken in facts of present case, to maintain confidentiality. Source of this power was Regulation 7(2)(h) of Insolvency and Bankruptcy Board of India (Insolvency Professionals) Regulations, 2016, read with paragraph 21 of First Schedule thereto. This could be in form of a non-disclosure agreement in which resolution professional could be indemnified in case information was not kept strictly confidential. [15]

5. Proviso to Section 21(2) clarified that, a director who was also a financial creditor who was a related party of corporate debtor shall not have any right of representation, participation, or voting in a meeting of committee of creditors. Directors, simplicitor, were not subject matter of proviso to Section 21(2), but only directors who were related parties of corporate debtor. It was only such persons who did not have any right of representation, participation, or voting in a meeting of committee of creditors. Therefore, contention that a director simplicitor would have right to get documents as against a director who was a financial creditor was not an argument that was based on proviso to Section 21(2), correctly read, as it referred only to a financial creditor who was a related party of corporate debtor. [16]

6. Time that had been utilized in present proceedings must be excluded from period of resolution process of corporate debtor as had been held in Arcelormittal India Private Limited v. Satish Kumar Gupta and Ors. Appellants would be given copies of all resolution plans submitted to CoC within a period of two weeks from date of this judgment. Resolution applicant in each of these cases would then convene a meeting of CoC within two weeks thereafter, which would include Appellants as participants. CoC would then deliberate on resolution plans afresh and either reject them or approve of them with requisite majority, after which, further procedure detailed in the Code and Regulations would be followed. NCLAT judgment was set aside. Appeal allowed. [18]

9

K. SASHIDHAR VS. INDIAN OVERSEAS BANK AND ORS. (05.02.2019 – SC)

Relevant Section: Section 33 & Section 34 of Insolvency and Bankruptcy Code, 2016

Hon'ble Judges/Coram: A.M. Khanwilkar and Ajay Rastogi, JJ.

Number of PDF Pages in Original Judgement: 40

Citation: AIR2019SC1329, II(2019)BC253(SC), [2019]148CLA497(SC), [2019]213CompCas356(SC), (2019)2CompLJ1(SC), 2019(2)CTC321, 2019(3)SCALE6, (2019)12SCC150, 2019 (8) SCJ 118, [2019]152SCL312(SC), MANU/SC/0189/2019

Case Note: Company - Rejection of resolution plan - Initiation of liquidation process - Challenge thereto - Sections 30, 31, 33, 61 of Insolvency and Bankruptcy Code, 2016 (I & B Code) - Appeals was against impugned order of NCLAT and High Court dismissing appeal filed by Appellant observing that, requirement of approval of resolution plan by vote of not less than 75% of voting share of financial creditors was mandatory -Whether resolution plan of concerned corporate debtor(s) had not been approved by requisite percent of voting share of financial creditors.

Appeal Dismissed

Facts: Present appeals had arisen from common judgment and order of National Company Law Appellate Tribunal (NCLAT), rendered in appeals filed in relation to insolvency resolution process under provisions of Insolvency and Bankruptcy Code, 2016 (I & B Code) concerning Kamineni Steel & Power India Pvt. Ltd. (KS & PIPL), having its registered office at Hyderabad, Telangana and Innoventive Industries Ltd. (IIL) having its registered office at Pune, Maharashtra. NCLAT affirmed order passed by National Company Law Tribunal, Mumbai Bench (NCLT Mumbai) recording rejection of resolution plan concerning IIL and directing initiation of liquidation process under Chapter III of Part II of the I & B Code. As regards KS & PIPL, NCLAT reversed decision of National Company Law Tribunal, Hyderabad (NCLT Hyderabad) which had approved its resolution plan and instead remanded proceedings to NCLT Hyderabad for initiation of liquidation process in terms of Section 33 and 34 of I & B Code. NCLAT held that as, in both cases, resolution plan did not garner support of not less than 75% of voting share of financial creditors constituting the Committee of Creditors (CoC) same stood rejected and thereby warranted initiation of liquidation process of concerned corporate debtor, namely, KS & PIPL and IIL. By impugned judgment NCLAT had held that, requirement of approval of resolution plan by vote of not less than 75% of voting share of financial creditors was mandatory and hence dismissed appeal preferred by Appellant. Aggrieved, said Appellant and workers' union of KS & PIPL had filed appeals against said decision of NCLAT and High Court respectively.

Hon'ble Apex Court held, while dismissing the appeal

1. Resolution plan concerning both corporate debtors, namely KS & PIPL and IIL was considered by concerned CoC in October 2017, and was approved by less than 75% of voting share of financial creditors. Inevitable consequences thereof were to treat proposed resolution plan as disapproved or deemed

to be rejected by dissenting financial creditors. Expression 'dissenting financial creditors, was defined in Regulation 2(1)(f) of Insolvency and Bankruptcy Board of India (Insolvency Resolution Process for Corporate Persons) Regulations, 2016, to mean financial creditors who voted against resolution plan approved by Committee. This definition came to be amended subsequently w.e.f. 1st January, 2018 to mean financial creditors who voted against resolution plan or abstained from voting for resolution plan, approved by Committee. [24]

2. Admittedly, in case of corporate debtor KS & PIPL, resolution plan, when it was put to vote in meeting of CoC held on 27th October, 2017, could garner approval of only 55.73% of voting share of financial creditors and even if subsequent approval accorded by email (by 10.94%) was taken into account, it did not fulfill requisite vote of not less than 75% of voting share of financial creditors. On other hand, resolution plan was expressly rejected by 15.15% in CoC meeting and later additionally by 11.82% by email. Thus, resolution plan was expressly rejected by not less than 25% of voting share of financial creditors. In such a case, resolution professional was under no obligation to submit resolution plan under Section 30(6) of I & B Code to adjudicating authority. Instead, it was a case to be proceeded by adjudicating authority under Section 33(1) of I & B Code. Similarly, in case of corporate debtor IIL, resolution plan received approval of only 66.57% of voting share of financial creditors and 33.43% voted against resolution plan. This being indisputable position, NCLAT opined that, resolution plan was deemed to be rejected by CoC and concomitant was to initiate liquidation process concerning two corporate debtors. [25]

3. According to resolution applicant and stakeholders supporting concerned resolution plan in respect of two corporate debtors, stipulation in Section 30(4) of I & B Code as applicable at relevant time in October 2017 was only directory and not mandatory. This argument was founded on expression "may" occurring in Section 30(4) of I & B Code. In that, word "may" was ascribable

to discretion of CoC-to approve resolution plan or not to approve same. Second part of said provision was significant, which stipulated requisite threshold of "not less than seventy five percent of voting share of financial creditors" to treat resolution plan as duly approved by CoC. That stipulation was quintessence and made mandatory for approval of resolution plan. Any other interpretation would result in rewriting of provision and doing violence to legislative intent. [26]

4. On a bare reading of provisions of I & B Code, it would appear that, remedy of appeal under Section 61(1) was against an "order passed by adjudicating authority (NCLT)". Indubitably, remedy of appeal including width of jurisdiction of appellate authority and grounds of appeal, was a creature of statute. Provisions investing jurisdiction and authority in NCLT or NCLAT had not made commercial decision exercised by CoC of not approving resolution plan or rejecting same, justiciable. This position was reinforced from limited grounds specified for instituting an appeal that too against an order "approving a resolution plan" under Section 31. First, that approved resolution plan was in contravention of provisions of any law for time being in force. Second, there had been material irregularity in exercise of powers "by resolution professional" during corporate insolvency resolution period. Third, debts owed to operational creditors had not been provided for in resolution plan in prescribed manner. Fourth, insolvency resolution plan costs had not been provided for repayment in priority to all other debts. Fifth, resolution plan did not comply with any other criteria specified by Board. Significantly, matters or grounds-be it under Section 30(2) or under Section-61(3) of I & B Code-were regarding testing validity of "approved" resolution plan by CoC; and not for approving resolution plan which had been disapproved or deemed to have been rejected by CoC in exercise of its business decision. [37]

5. Indubitably, inquiry in such an appeal would be limited to power exercisable by resolution professional under Section 30(2) of I

& B Code or, at best, by adjudicating authority (NCLT) under Section 31(2) read with 31(1) of I & B Code. No other inquiry would be permissible. Further, jurisdiction bestowed upon appellate authority (NCLAT) was also expressly circumscribed. It could examine challenge only in relation to grounds specified in Section 61(3) of I & B Code, which was limited to matters "other than" enquiry into autonomy or commercial wisdom of dissenting financial creditors. Thus, prescribed authorities (NCLT/NCLAT) had been endowed with limited jurisdiction as specified in I & B Code and not to act as a Court of equity or exercise plenary powers. [38]

6. Neither adjudicating authority (NCLT) nor appellate authority (NCLAT) had been endowed with jurisdiction to reverse commercial wisdom of dissenting financial creditors and that too on specious ground that, it was only an opinion of minority financial creditors. Fact that substantial or majority percent of financial creditors had accorded approval to resolution plan would be of no avail, unless approval was by a vote of not less than 75% (after amendment of 2018 w.e.f. 06.06.2018, 66%) of voting share of financial creditors. Action of liquidation process postulated in Chapter-III of I & B Code, was avoidable, only if approval of resolution plan was by a vote of not less than 75% (as in October, 2017) of voting share of financial creditors. Conversely, legislative intent was to uphold opinion or hypothesis of minority dissenting financial creditors. That must prevail, if it was not less than specified percent (25% in October, 2017; and now after amendment w.e.f. 06.06.2018, 44%). Inevitable outcome of voting by not less than requisite percent of voting share of financial creditors to disapprove proposed resolution plan, de jure, entailed in its deemed rejection. [39]

7. Threshold of voting share of dissenting financial creditors for rejecting resolution plan was way below simple majority mark, namely not less than 25% (and even after amendment w.e.f. 06.06.2018, 44%). Thus, scrutiny of resolution plan was required to pass through litmus test of not less than requisite (75% or

66% as may be applicable) of voting share-a strict regime. That meant resolution plan must appear, to not less than requisite voting share of financial creditors, to be an overall credible plan, capable of achieving timelines specified in Code generally, assuring successful revival of corporate debtor and disavowing endless speculation. [40]

8. Scope of enquiry and grounds on which decision of "approval" of resolution plan by CoC could be interfered with by adjudicating authority (NCLT), had been set out in Section 31(1) read with Section 30(2) and by appellate tribunal (NCLAT) under Section 32 read with Section 61(3) of I & B Code. No corresponding provision had been envisaged by legislature to empower resolution professional, adjudicating authority (NCLT) or for that matter appellate authority (NCLAT), to reverse "commercial decision" of CoC much less of dissenting financial creditors for not supporting the proposed resolution plan. Whereas, from legislative history there was contra indication that, commercial or business decisions of financial creditors were not open to any judicial review by adjudicating authority or appellate authority. [42]

9. In I & B Code and Regulations framed thereunder as applicable in October 2017, there was no need for dissenting financial creditors to record reasons for disapproving or rejecting a resolution plan. Further, there was no provision in I & B Code which empowered adjudicating authority (NCLT) to oversee justness of approach of dissenting financial creditors in rejecting proposed resolution plan or to engage in judicial review thereof. Concededly, inquiry by resolution professional preceded consideration of resolution plan by CoC. Resolution professional was not required to express his opinion on matters within domain of financial creditor(s), to approve or reject resolution plan, under Section 30(4) of I & B Code. Adjudicating Authority (NCLT) might cause an enquiry into "approved" resolution plan on limited grounds referred to in Section 30(2) read with Section 31(1) of I & B Code. It could not make any other inquiry nor was competent to issue

any direction in relation to exercise of commercial wisdom of financial creditors-be it for approving, rejecting or abstaining, as case might be. Even inquiry before Appellate Authority (NCLAT) was limited to grounds under Section 61(3) of I & B Code. It did not postulate jurisdiction to undertake scrutiny of justness of opinion expressed by financial creditors at time of voting. [44]

10. Since none of grounds available under Section 30(2) or Section 61(3) of I & B Code were attracted in fact situation of present case, Adjudicating Authority (NCLT) as well as Appellate Authority (NCLAT) had no other option but to record that, proposed resolution plan concerning respective corporate debtor (KS & PIPL and IIL) stood rejected. Further, as no alternative resolution plan was approved by requisite percent of voting share of financial creditors before expiry of statutory period of 270 days, inevitable sequel was to pass an order directing initiation of liquidation process against concerned corporate debtor in manner specified in Chapter III of I & B Code. [45]

11. Change brought about by Insolvency and Bankruptcy Code (Amendment) Act, 2017 was insertion of words "after considering its feasibility and viability, and such other requirements as might be specified by the Board". In addition, three provisos had been added to Sub-section (4). As regards insertion of above quoted words in Sub-section (4), that did not alter requirement regarding approval of a resolution plan, by a vote of not less than 75% of voting share of financial creditors. Amendment was only to declare that, financial creditors ought to consider feasibility and viability and such other requirements as might be specified by Board, while exercising their option on resolution plan-to approve or not to approve same. [47]

12. Amended provision merely restated as to what financial creditors were expected to bear in mind whilst expressing their choice during consideration of proposal for approval of a resolution plan. No more and no less. In present cases, there was nothing to indicate as to which other requirements specified by Board at relevant time had not been fulfilled by dissenting financial

creditors. Board established under Section 188 of I & B Code could perform powers and functions specified in Section 196 of I & B Code. That did not empower Board to specify requirements for exercising commercial decisions by financial creditors in matters of approval of resolution plan or liquidation process. [48]

13. In present case, however, amendment under consideration pertaining to Section 30(4), was to modify voting share threshold for decisions of the CoC and could not be treated as clarificatory in nature. It changed qualifying standards for reckoning decision of CoC concerning process of approval of a resolution plan. Rights/obligations crystallized between parties and, in particular, dissenting financial creditors in October 2017, in terms of governing provisions could be divested or undone only by a law made in that behalf by legislature. There was no indication either in report of Committee or in Amendment Act of 2018 that, legislature intended to undo decisions of the CoC already taken prior to 6th day of June, 2018. [58]

14. Amendment to Regulation 39 could not have retrospective effect so as to impact decision of CoC of concerned corporate debtor - taken before amendment of said Regulation. There was no indication in Code as amended or Regulations to suggest that, as a consequence of this amendment decisions already taken by concerned CoC prior to 3rd July, 2018 be treated as deemed to have been vitiated or for that matter, necessitating reversion of proposal to CoC for recording reasons, that too beyond the statutory period of 270 days. A new life could not be infused in resolution plan which did not fructify within statutory period, by such circuitous route. [60]

15. As regards application by resolution applicant for taking his revised resolution plan on record, same was also devoid of merits as it was not open to Adjudicating Authority to entertain a revised resolution plan after expiry of statutory period of 270 days. Accordingly, no fault could be found with NCLAT for not entertaining such application. [64]

16. NCLAT had justly concluded in impugned decision that, resolution plan of concerned corporate debtor(s) had not been approved by requisite percent of voting share of financial creditors; and in absence of any alternative resolution plan presented within statutory period of 270 days, inevitable sequel was to initiate liquidation process under Section 33 of Code. [66]

17. Appeals dismissed. [67]

> **Legal Latin Terms Group 5**
>
> de novo - Anew or afresh
>
> de son tort - Of his own wrong
>
> dies non - Not a day
>
> duces tecum - bring with you
>
> dum bene se gesserit - While he shall conduct himself, during good behavior
>
> e converso - Conversely or on the other hand
>
> en banc - All judges present on the bench to hear a case
>
> eo instanti - Upon the instant
>
> erratum - Error
>
> et alii - And others
>
> et sequentia - And as follows

10

EMBASSY PROPERTY DEVELOPMENTS PVT. LTD. VS. STATE OF KARNATAKA AND ORS. (03.12.2019 – SC)

Relevant Section: Sections 6, 7, 61 and 65(1) of Insolvency and Bankruptcy Code, 2016

Hon'ble Judges/Coram: Rohinton Fali Nariman, Aniruddha Bose and V. Ramasubramanian, JJ.

Number of PDF Pages in Original Judgement: 21

Citation: 2020(1)ALT42, I(2020)BC277(SC), [2019]153CLA366(SC), 2020(1)CTC853, 2020-3-LW269, (2020)1MLJ65, 2019(17)SCALE37, [2020]157SCL445(SC), MANU/SC/1661/2019

Case Note: Company - Supplemental lease deed - Jurisdiction thereto - Sections 6, 61 and 65(1) of Insolvency and Bankruptcy Code, 2016 - Twelfth Respondent, claiming to be Financial Creditor, moved application before National Company Law Tribunal (NCLT) under Section 7 of Insolvency and Bankruptcy Code, 2016 against Corporate Debtor - NCLT ordered commencement of Corporate Insolvency Resolution Process and appointed Interim Resolution Professional - Corporate Debtor held mining lease granted by Government was to expire after certain period - Interim Resolution Professional appointed addressed letter to Director of Mines, seeking benefit of deemed extension of lease - Government passed order rejecting proposal for deemed extension - Resolution Professional moved application before NCLT praying for setting aside order of Government - NCLT set aside order of rejection and directing Government to execute Supplemental Lease Deeds - Challenging order of NCLT, Government moved writ petition before High Court - High Court granted stay of operation of direction contained in impugned order of Tribunal - Hence, present appeal - Whether High Court ought to interfere with order passed by NCLT in proceeding under Insolvency and Bankruptcy Code, 2016 and questions of fraud could be inquired into by NCLT/NCLAT in proceedings initiated under Insolvency and Bankruptcy Code, 2016. - Hence, the High Court was justified in entertaining the writ petition and we see no reason to interfere with the decision of the High Court.

The appeals are dismissed.

Facts: The twelfth Respondent, claiming to be a Financial Creditor, moved an application before the NCLT under Section 7 of the Insolvency and Bankruptcy Code, 2016 against the Corporate Debtor. The NCLT admitted the application, ordered the commencement of the Corporate Insolvency Resolution Process and appointed an Interim Resolution Professional. The Corporate Debtor held a mining lease granted by the Government, which was to expire after a certain period. Though a notice for premature termination of the lease had already been issued, on the allegation of violation of statutory Rules and the terms and conditions of the lease deed, no order of termination had been passed till the date of initiation of the Corporate Insolvency Resolution Process (CIRP). The Interim Resolution Professional appointed by NCLT wrote a letter to the Director of Mines and Geology, seeking the benefit of deemed extension of the lease. The Government passed an order rejecting the proposal for deemed extension, on the ground that the Corporate Debtor had contravened not only the terms and conditions of the Lease Deed but also the provisions of Rule 37 of the Mineral Concession Rules, 1960 and Rule 24 of the Minerals Rules, 2016. The Resolution Professional moved a Miscellaneous Application before the NCLT, praying for setting aside the Order of the Government. The NCLT passed an Order allowing the Miscellaneous Application, setting aside the order of rejection and directing the Government to execute Supplemental Lease Deeds. Challenging the Order of the NCLT, the Government moved a writ petition before the High Court. The High Court, granted a stay of operation of the direction contained in the impugned Order of the Tribunal.

Hon'ble Apex Court held, while dismissing the appeal:

i. After the filing of the first writ petition, the Government passed an order rejecting the claim. Therefore the Resolution Professional, representing the Corporate Debtor filed a memo before the High Court seeking withdrawal of the writ petition with liberty to file a fresh writ petition. However the High Court, while dismissing the writ petition by order was little considerate and it disposed of the writ petition as withdrawn with liberty to take recourse to appropriate remedies in accordance with law. Perhaps taking advantage of this liberty, the Resolution Applicant moved the NCLT against the order of rejection passed by the Government. If NCLT was not considered by the Resolution Professional, in the first instance, to be empowered to issue a declaration of deemed extension of lease, this court fail to understand how NCLT could be considered to have the power of judicial review over the order of rejection. [42]

ii. The fact that the Government agreed in the second writ petition to go back to the NCLT and contest the Miscellaneous Application filed by the Resolution Professional, would not tantamount to conceding the jurisdiction of NCLT. In any case a tribunal which was the creature of a statute could not be clothed with a jurisdiction, by any concession made by a party. [43]

iii. Therefore, NCLT did not have jurisdiction to entertain an application against the Government for a direction to execute Supplemental Lease Deeds for the extension of the mining lease. Since NCLT chose to exercise a jurisdiction not vested in it in law, the High Court was justified in entertaining the writ petition, on the basis that NCLT was coram non judice. [45]

iv. Even fraudulent tradings carried on by the Corporate Debtor during the insolvency resolution, could be inquired into by the Adjudicating Authority under Section 66. Section 69 makes an officer of the corporate debtor and the corporate debtor liable for punishment, for carrying on transactions with a view to defraud creditors. Therefore, NCLT was vested with the power to inquire into (i) fraudulent initiation of proceedings as well as (ii) fraudulent transactions. It was significant to note that Section 65(1) deals with a situation where CIRP is initiated fraudulently for any purpose other than for the resolution of insolvency or liquidation. [50]

v. Therefore, if, as contended by the Government, the CIRP had been initiated by one and the same person taking different avatars, not for the genuine purpose of resolution of insolvency or liquidation, but for the collateral purpose of cornering the mine and the mining lease, the same would fall squarely within the mischief addressed by Section 65(1). Therefore, it was clear that NCLT had jurisdiction to enquire into allegations of fraud. As a corollary, NCLAT would also have jurisdiction. Hence, fraudulent initiation of CIRP could not be a ground to bypass the alternative remedy of appeal provided in Section 61 of Act. [51]

11

MAHARASHTRA SEAMLESS LIMITED VS. PADMANABHAN VENKATESH AND ORS. (22.01.2020 – SC)

Relevant Section: Insolvency And Bankruptcy Code, 2016 - Section 12-A

Hon'ble Judges/Coram: Rohinton Fali Nariman, Aniruddha Bose and V. Ramasubramanian, JJ.

Number of PDF Pages in Original Judgement: 18

Citations: I(2020)BC488(SC), [2020]154CLA280(SC), 2020 (2) SCJ 522, [2020]158SCL567(SC), MANU/SC/0066/2020

Case Note: Company - Resolution plan - Approval of - Sections 30(2), 30(4) and 31(1) of Insolvency and Bankruptcy Code, 2016 - Proceedings of Corporate Insolvency Resolution Process (CIRP) was initiated - Application was filed before Adjudicating Authority by Resolution Professional in which he sought approval of resolution plan - Adjudicating Authority directing Resolution Professional to re-determine liquidation value of corporate debtor - Revised valuation of corporate debtor was made by enhancing same - Order of Adjudicating Authority was appealed against by Appellant before Appellate Tribunal - Before disposal of Company Appeal, resolution professional had filed application before Adjudicating Authority seeking approval of resolution plan - Adjudicating Authority approved resolution plan upon considering Section 31 of 2016 Code - Appellate Tribunal found reasoning of Adjudicating Authority flawed and Resolution Plan, as approved by Adjudicating Authority was against Section 30(2) (b) of Code - Hence, present appeal - Whether Adjudicating Authority erred in directing successful Resolution Applicant to enhance their fund inflow upfront.-

Appeal Allowed

Facts: The Corporate Insolvency Resolution Process (CIRP) was initiated involving, the corporate debtor. The application was filed before the Adjudicating Authority by the Resolution Professional in which he sought approval of the resolution plan. That application was disposed of by the Adjudicating Authority by an order inter-alia, directing the Resolution Professional to re-determine the liquidation value of the corporate debtor by taking into consideration the first and second valuation of registered valuers. The Revised valuation of the corporate debtor was made, enhancing the same. In its meeting, the Committee took into consideration the revised valuation and on majority voting approved again the resolution plan of Appellant. The order of the Adjudicating Authority was appealed against by Appellant before the Appellate Tribunal. Before disposal of Company Appeal, the resolution professional had filed an application before the Adjudicating Authority seeking approval of the resolution plan as per the decision in the meeting of the committee. The order of the Adjudicating Authority was issued approving the resolution plan upon considering Section 31 of the 2016 Code. The Appellate Tribunal, however, found the reasoning of the Adjudicating Authority flawed and directed successful Resolution Applicant to enhance their fund inflow upfront.

Hon'ble Apex Court held, while allowing the appeal:

i. No provision in the Code or Regulations has been brought to our notice under which the bid of any Resolution Applicant had to match liquidation value arrived at in the manner provided in Clause 35 of the Insolvency and Bankruptcy Board of India Regulations, 2016. [26]

ii. The object behind prescribing such valuation process was to assist the CoC to take decision on a resolution plan properly. Once, a resolution plan was approved by the CoC, the statutory mandate on the Adjudicating Authority under Section 31(1) of the Code is to ascertain that a resolution plan meets the requirement of Sub-sections (2) and (4) of Section 30 thereof. There was no breach of the said provisions in the order of the Adjudicating Authority in approving the resolution plan. [27]

iii. The Appellate Authority had proceeded on equitable perception rather than commercial wisdom. On the face of it, release of assets at a value twenty percent below its liquidation value arrived at by the valuers seems inequitable. The Court ought to cede ground to the commercial wisdom of the creditors rather than assess the resolution plan on the basis of quantitative analysis. Such was the scheme of the Code. Section 31(1) of the Code lays down in clear terms that for final approval of a resolution plan, the Adjudicating Authority has to be satisfied that the requirement of Sub-section (2) of Section 30 of the Code has been complied with. The proviso to Section 31(1) of the Code stipulates the other point on which an Adjudicating Authority has to be satisfied. That factor was that the resolution plan has provisions for its implementation. The scope of interference by the Adjudicating Authority in limited judicial review had been laid down in the case of Essar Steel. The case of Appellant in their appeal was that they want to run the company and infuse more funds. In such circumstances, the Appellate Authority ought not to have interfered with the order of the Adjudicating Authority in directing the successful Resolution Applicant to enhance their fund inflow upfront. [28]

12

DUNCANS INDUSTRIES LTD. VS. A.J. AGROCHEM (04.10.2019 – SC)

Relevant Section: Insolvency And Bankruptcy Code, 2016 - Section 9; Tea Act, 1953 - Section 16G(1)(c)

Hon'ble Judges/Coram: Arun Mishra, M.R. Shah and B.R. Gavai, JJ.

Number of PDF Pages in Original Judgement: 12

Citation: AIR2019SC5472, 2020(1)ALD179, IV(2019)BC456(SC), [2019]153CLA44(SC), [2019]217CompCas320(SC), (2019)4CompLJ438(SC), 2020(2)CTC842, (2019)7MLJ748, 2019(13)SCALE535, (2019)9SCC725, [2019]156SCL478(SC), (2020)1WBLR(SC)169, 2019 (4) WLN 121 (SC), MANU/SC/1385/2019

Case Note: Banking - Maintainability of application - Section 9 of Insolvency and Bankruptcy Code, 2016 - Respondent was operational creditor of Appellant - According to Respondent-operational creditor, sum was due and payable by Appellant-corporate debtor to Respondent-operational creditor - Respondent initiated proceedings against Appellant-corporate debtor before Tribunal under Section 9 of Code - Tribunal held that in view of statutory provisions under Section 16G of Tea Act, 1953 and as prior consent of Central Government had not been obtained, proceedings under Section 9 of

Code shall not be maintainable - In appeal, Appellate Tribunal had reversed order passed by Tribunal and had held that Respondent's application under Section 9 of Code would be maintainable even without consent of Central Government in terms of Section 16G of Act - Hence, present appeal - Whether Respondent's application under Section 9 of Code would be maintainable even without consent of Central Government in terms of Section 16G of Act.-

Appeal Dismissed

Facts: The Respondent was an operational creditor of the Appellant. It used to supply pesticides, insecticides, herbicides etc. to the Appellant. According to the Respondent-operational creditor, a sum was due and payable by the Appellant-corporate debtor to the Respondent-operational creditor. That the Respondent initiated the proceedings against the Appellant-corporate debtor before the Tribunal under Section 9 of the IBC. The Tribunal held that in view of the statutory provisions under Section 16G of the Tea Act and as the prior consent of the Central Government had not been obtained, the proceedings under Section 9 of the IBC shall not be maintainable. In an appeal, the Appellate Tribunal held that the Respondent's application under Section 9 of the IBC would be maintainable even without the consent of the Central Government in terms of Section 16G of the Tea Act.

Hon'ble Apex Court held, while dismissing the appeal:

i. It was true that by notification issued under Section 16E of the Tea Act, the Central Government authorised the Tea Board to take over the management or the control of the seven tea estates mentioned in the said notification. However, the Appellant challenged the said notification before the High Court and the Single Judge of the High Court dismissed the said petition. However, in an appeal, the Division Bench of the High Court had permitted the Appellant-corporate debtor to continue with the management of the said tea estates. Therefore, in effect, the Appellant had been continued to be in management and control of the tea estates, despite the notification under Section 16E of Act. At this stage, it was required to be noted that notification under Section 16E of the Tea Act was issued by the Central Government and the Central Government authorised the Tea Board to take steps to take over the management and control of the seven tea estates, having satisfied that the said seven tea gardens were being managed by the Appellant in a manner highly detrimental to the tea industry and public interest. Despite the same, very surprisingly, by an interim arrangement, the Division Bench of the High Court had handed over the management and control of the seven tea gardens to the Appellant, because of whose mis-management, it had deteriorated the condition of the tea gardens run by the Appellant. Be that as it may, the fact remains that, pursuant to the interim arrangement/order passed by the Division Bench of the High Court, the Appellant-corporate debtor is continued to be in management and control of the seven tea gardens and they are running the tea gardens. Therefore, in the facts and circumstances of the case, and more particularly when, despite the notification under Section 16E of the Tea Act, the Appellant-corporate debtor was continued to be in management and control of the tea gardens/units and are running the tea gardens as if the notification dated under Section 16E had not been issued, Section 16G of the Tea Act, more particularly Section 16G(1)(c) of Act, shall not be applicable at all. On a fair reading of Section 16G of the Tea Act, it was found that Section 16G of the Tea Act shall be applicable only in a case where the actual management of a tea undertaking or tea unit owned by a company had been taken over by any person or body of persons authorised by the Central Government under the Tea Act. Therefore, taking over the actual management and control by the Central Government or by any person or body of persons authorised by the Central Government is sine qua non before Section 16G of the Tea Act was made applicable. Therefore, Section 16G(1)(c) of Act shall not be applicable at all, as the Appellant-corporate debtor was continued to be in management and control of the tea units/gardens. [7.1]

ii. Section 16G(1)(c) of Act refers to the proceeding for winding up of such company or for the appointment of receiver in respect thereof. Therefore, as such, the proceedings under Section 9 of the Code shall not be limited and/or restricted to winding up and/or appointment of receiver only. The winding up/liquidation of the company shall be the last resort and only on an eventuality when the corporate insolvency resolution process fails. As observed by this Court in Swiss Ribbons Pvt. Ltd., the primary focus of the legislation while enacting the IBC was to ensure revival and continuation of the corporate debtor by protecting the corporate debtor from its own management and from a corporate debt by liquidation and such corporate insolvency resolution process is to be completed in a time-bound manner. Therefore, the entire corporate insolvency resolution process as such could not be equated with winding up proceedings. Therefore, considering Section 238 of the IBC, which was a subsequent Act to the Tea Act, 1953, shall be applicable and the provisions of the IBC shall have an over-riding effect over the Tea Act, 1953. Any other view would frustrate the object and purpose of the IBC. If the submission on behalf of the Appellant that before initiation of proceedings under Section 9 of the IBC, the consent of the Central Government as provided under Section 16G(1)(c) of the Tea Act was to be obtained, in that case, the main object and purpose of the IBC, namely, to complete the corporate insolvency resolution process in a time-bound manner, shall be frustrated. The sum and substance of the discussion would be that the provisions of the IBC would have an over-riding effect over the Tea Act, 1953 and that no prior consent of the Central Government before initiation of the proceedings under Section 7 or Section 9 of the IBC would be required and even without such consent of the Central Government, the insolvency proceedings under Section 7 or Section 9 of the IBC initiated by the operational creditor shall be maintainable. [7.4]

13

MUNICIPAL CORPORATION OF GREATER MUMBAI (MCGM) VS. ABHILASH LAL AND ORS. (15.11.2019 – SC)

Relevant Section: Insolvency And Bankruptcy Code, 2016 - Section 238; Mumbai Municipal Corporation Act, 1888 - Section 92; Section 92A

Hon'ble Judges/Coram: Arun Mishra, Vineet Saran and S. Ravindra Bhat, JJ.

Number of PDF Pages in Original Judgement: 21

Citation: I(2020)BC342(SC), 2020(1)BomCR320, [2020]155CLA5(SC), 2020(1)CTC555, 2019(16)SCALE507, [2020]157SCL477(SC), MANU/SC/1580/2019

Case Note: Company - Resolution plan - Validity of - Sections 92,92A and 238 of Insolvency and Bankruptcy Code, 2016 - Appellant owns inter alia, lands and by contract company agreed to develop these lands and construct hospital - On strength of contract, company had borrowed from banks and financial institutions - Said company inability to repay its debts led to initiation of insolvency proceedings and first Respondent was appointed as Resolution Professional - As result of RFP published, resolution plan was approved by Committee of Creditors - Application for approval of resolution plan was filed before National Company Law Tribunal which stand approved - On appeal, Appellate Tribunal rejected Appellants plea with respect to resolution plan approved by Company Law Tribunal under provisions of that Code - Hence, present appeal - Whether impugned order pertaining to approval of resolution plan by National Company Law Tribunal was sustainable.

Appeal Allowed

Facts: Appellant owns inter alia lands and by a contract one company agreed to develop these lands and construct a hospital. On the strength of the contract, said company had borrowed from banks and financial institutions. It had created security by way of mortgage of the said lands, citing clause of contract, which enabled the creation of such encumbrances. The Company inability to repay its debts led to the initiation of insolvency proceedings and the first Respondent was appointed as the Resolution Professional. As a result of the RFP published, a resolution plan was approved by Committee of Creditors. The Application for approval of the resolution plan was filed before National Company Law Tribunal which stand approved. Appeal was filed before Appellate Tribunal against said order, Appellate Tribunal rejected Appellants plea with respect to resolution plan approved by Company Law Tribunal under provisions of that Code.

Hon'ble Apex Court held, while allowing the appeal:

i. It was evident from a plain reading of Section 92(c), that the Commissioner was empowered to, with the sanction of the corporation, lease, sell or otherwise convey any immovable property belonging to the corporation. It was not in dispute that the original contract contemplated the fulfilment of some important conditions, including firstly, the completion of the hospital project within a time frame; and secondly, timely payment of annual lease rentals. It was a matter of record that the hospital project was scheduled to be completed. Appellant cites the contract to urge that within a month of this event, i.e.

completion of the hospital, a lease deed had to be executed. This event never took place. Therefore, the terms of the contract remained, in the opinion of the court, an agreement to enter into a lease, it did not per se confer any right or interest, except that in the event of Appellant's failure or omission to register the lease, it could be sued for specific performance of the agreement, and compelled to execute a lease deed. That event did not occur, company did not complete construction of the hospital. Apparently, it did not even fulfill its commitment, or pay annual lease rentals. In these circumstances, Appellant was constrained to issue a show cause notice before the insolvency resolution process began, and before the moratorium was declared by NCLT. According to MCGM, in terms of the contract, even the agreement stood terminated due to default by company. This Court did not propose to comment on that issue, as that was contentious and no finding has been recorded by either the adjudicating authority or the NCLAT. [36]

ii. Section 238 could not be read as overriding the Appellant's right - indeed its public duty-to control and regulate how its properties are to be dealt with. That exists in Sections 92 and 92A of the MMC Act. This Court was of opinion that Section 238 could be of importance when the properties and assets were of a debtor and not when a third party like the Appellant was involved. Therefore, in the absence of approval in terms of Section 92 and 92A of the MMC Act, the adjudicating authority could not have overridden MCGM's objections and enabled the creation of a fresh interest in respect of its properties and lands. No doubt, the resolution plans talk of seeking MCGM's approval they also acknowledge the liabilities of the corporate debtor, equally, however, there are proposals which envision the creation of charge or securities in respect of Appellant's properties. Nevertheless, the authorities under the Code could not have precluded the control that Appellant undoubtedly had, under law, to deal with its properties and the land in question-which undeniably were public properties. The resolution plan therefore, would be a serious impediment to Appellant's independent plans to ensure that public health amenities were developed in the manner it chooses, and for which fresh approval under the MMC Act may be forthcoming for a separate scheme formulated by that corporation. [47]

iii. The impugned order and the order of the NCLT could not stand, they were hereby set aside. [49]

Legal Latin Terms Group 6

et ux - And wife

et vir - And husband

ex delicto - Arising from a tort

ex gratia - As a matter of favor

ex officio - From office, by virtue of his office

ex parte - By or for one party only

ex post facto - After the fact

facto - In fact, in or by the law

felonice - Feloniously

fiat - Let it be done, a short order that a thing be done

fieri - To be made up, to become

14

JAIPRAKASH ASSOCIATES LTD. AND ORS. VS. IDBI BANK LTD. AND ORS. (06.11.2019 – SC)

Relevant Section: Insolvency And Bankruptcy Code, 2016 - Section 29A

Hon'ble Judges/Coram: A.M. Khanwilkar and Dinesh Maheshwari, JJ.

Number of PDF Pages in Original Judgement: 11

Citation: I(2020)BC391(SC), [2019]153CLA141(SC), (2020)3MLJ247, 2019(14)SCALE740, (2020)3SCC328, 2020 (2) SCJ 638, [2019]156SCL782(SC), MANU/SC/1512/2019

Case Note: Company - Clarificatory application - Exclusion of period - Respondent-Bank filed application before National Company Law Tribunal (NCLT) for excluding period of pendency of application for clarification regarding manner of counting votes of concerned financial creditors from period of two hundred seventy days of Corporate Insolvency Resolution Process (CIRP) - While said application was pending, NCLT called upon authorities, representatives of allottees to file their reply on necessity to proceed further with CIRP, for considering resolution plan received from concerned bidder, subject to outcome of pending application - Respondent Bank, feeling aggrieved by opinion expressed by NCLT to proceed further with CIRP despite pending clarificatory motions before Appellate Tribunal, including application to exclude period during clarificatory application from total period of two hundred seventy days of CIRP - Appellate Tribunal excluded period during clarificatory application for purpose of counting two hundred seventy days Corporate Resolution Process period and issued consequential directions - Hence, present appeal - Whether Appellate Tribunal erred in excluding period of clarificatory application for purpose of counting two hundred seventy days CRP period.

Disposed off

Facts: The Respondent Bank filed an application before the National Company Law Tribunal (NCLT) for excluding the period of pendency of the application for clarification regarding the manner of counting votes of the concerned financial creditors from the period of 270 days of Corporate Insolvency Resolution Process (CIRP). While the said application was pending, NCLT by order called upon the authorities, representatives of the allottees and Ors. to file their reply on the necessity to proceed further with the CIRP in accordance with law, for considering the resolution plan received from the concerned bidder, subject to the outcome of the pending application. The Bank, feeling aggrieved by the opinion expressed by the NCLT to proceed further with the CIRP despite pending clarificatory motions before the NCLT/NCLAT respectively, including the application to exclude the period during the clarificatory application from the total period of two hundred seventy days of the CIRP, assailed the order passed by the NCLT. The Appellate Tribunal excluded period during clarificatory application for purpose of counting two hundred seventy days Corporate Resolution Process period and issued consequential directions.

Hon'ble Apex Court held, while disposing off the appeal:

i. An extraordinary situation had arisen because of the constant experimentation which went about at different level due to lack of clarity on matters crucial to the decision making process of Committee of Creditors (CoC). Besides that, in view of the recent legislative changes, the scope of resolution plan stands expanded which may now include provision for restructuring the corporate debtor including by way of merger, amalgamation and demerger and more so the power bestowed on the CoC to consider not only the feasibility and viability of the resolution plan but also the manner of distribution proposed, which may take into account the order of priority amongst the creditors. Additionally, the recently inserted Section 12A enables the adjudicating authority to allow the withdrawal of an application filed under Section 7 or Section 9 or Section 10, on an application made by the applicant with the approval of ninety percent voting share of the CoC. Similarly, Sub-clause (7) of Regulation 36B dealing with the request for resolution plans unambiguously postulates that the Resolution Professional may, with the approval of the Committee, reissue request for resolution plans, if the resolution plans received in response to earlier request are not satisfactory, subject to the condition that the request is made to all prospective resolution applicants in the final list. In the present case, finally only two bidders had participated and submitted their resolution plan which was placed before the CoC and stated to have been rejected. However, applying the principle underlying Regulation 36B(7), deem it appropriate to permit the IRP to reissue request for resolution plans to the two bidders and/or to call upon them to submit revised resolution plan(s), which could be then placed before the CoC for its due consideration. [16]

ii. There was unanimity amongst all the parties appearing before this Court including the resolution applicant that liquidation of company must be eschewed and instead an attempt be made to salvage the situation by finding out some viable arrangement which would subserve the interests of all concerned. [17]

iii. This court must exercise plenary powers to make an attempt to revive the corporate debtor (AIL), lest it is exposed to liquidation process under Chapter III of Part II of the I & B Code. This court inclined to do so because the project had been implemented in part and out of over twenty thousand home buyers, a substantial number of them have been put in possession and the remaining work is in progress and in some cases at an advanced stage of completion. In this backdrop, it would be in the interest of all concerned to accept a viable plan reflecting the recent legislative changes. [18]

iv. Therefore, deem it just, proper and expedient to issue directions under Article 142 of the Constitution of India to all concerned to reckon ninety days extended period from the date of this order instead of the date of commencement of the Insolvency and Bankruptcy Code (Amendment) Act, 2019. That means, in terms of this order, the CIRP concerning company shall be completed within a period of ninety days from today. [19]

Legal Latin Terms Group 7

fieri facias - Writ directing a sheriff to reduce a judgment debtor's property to money

flagrante delicto - In the very act of committing the crime

forum non conveniens - Power to decline jurisdiction over a case and have it tried elsewhere

gravis - Serious, of importance

habeas corpus - Writ commanded to the custodian of a person to produce the body now

habendum clause - The part of a deed beginning "to have and to hold" and defining ownership

honorarium - Fee, gift or compensation from gratitude

idem - The same as above (id.)

idem sonans - To have the same sound, as in names sounding alike but spelled differently

in curia - In court

15

ANAND RAO KORADA VS. VARSHA FABRICS (P) LTD. AND ORS. (18.11.2019 – SC)

Relevant Section: Insolvency And Bankruptcy Code, 2016 - Section 231; Section 238

Hon'ble Judges/Coram: Indu Malhotra and R. Subhash Reddy, JJ.

Number of PDF Pages in Original Judgement: 7

Citation: AIR2020SC222, 2020(2)ALD251, [2019]153CLA269(SC), 2019(16)SCALE499, [2020]157SCL350(SC), MANU/SC/1602/2019

Case Note: Company - Auction - Validity thereof - Sections 7, 13, 15, 231 and 238 of Insolvency and Bankruptcy Code, 2016 - Financial Creditor filed petition under Section 7 of Code before National Company Law Tribunal for initiation of Corporate Insolvency Resolution Process (CIRP) against Corporate Debtor-Respondent No. 4, since it had committed default in paying financial debt - Tribunal admitted insolvency petition, and declared moratorium in accordance with provisions of Sections 13 and 15 of IBC - Appellant was appointed as Insolvency Resolution Professional - During pendency of moratorium, High Court High Court passed orders for carrying out auction of assets of Respondent No. 4-Company - Hence, present appeal - Whether High Court erred in passing orders for carrying out auction of assets of Respondent No. 4-Company.

Appeal Allowed

Facts: A Financial Creditor filed a Petition under Section 7 of the IBC, 2016 before the National Company Law Tribunal, for initiation of the Corporate Insolvency Resolution Process (CIRP) against the Corporate Debtor-Respondent No. 4, since it had committed a default in paying the financial debt. The NCLT admitted the insolvency petition, and declared a moratorium in accordance with the provisions of Sections 13 and 15 of the IBC. The moratorium was declared for the purpose referred to in Section 14 of the IBC. The Appellant herein was appointed as the Insolvency Resolution Professional. During the pendency of the moratorium, the High Court passed orders for carrying out auction of assets of Respondent No. 4-Company.

Hon'ble Apex Court held, while allowing the appeal:

i. Section 238 gives an overriding effect to the IBC over all other laws. The provisions of the IBC vest exclusive jurisdiction on the NCLT and the NCLAT to deal with all issues pertaining to the insolvency process of a corporate debtor, and the mode and manner of disposal of its assets. [7]

ii. Section 231 of the IBC bars the jurisdiction of civil courts in respect of any matter in which the Adjudicating Authority i.e. the NCLT or the NCLAT is empowered by the Code to pass any Order. [8]

iii. In view of the provisions of the IBC, the High Court ought not to have proceeded with the auction of the property of the Corporate Debtor-Respondent No. 4, once the proceedings under the IBC had commenced, and an Order declaring moratorium was passed by the NCLT. The High Court passed the impugned Interim Orders after the CIRP had commenced in this case. The moratorium having been declared by the NCLT, the

High Court was not justified in passing the Orders for carrying out auction of the assets of the Respondent No. 4-Company i.e. the Corporate Debtor before the NCLT. The subject matter of the auction proceedings before the High Court was a vast chunk of land, including Railway lines and buildings. If the assets of the Respondent No. 4-Company are alienated during the pendency of the proceedings under the IBC, it would seriously jeopardise the interest of all the stakeholders. As a consequence, set aside the impugned Interim Orders passed by the High Court, as parallel proceedings with respect to the main issue could not take place in the High Court. The sale or liquidation of the assets of Respondent No. 4 would now be governed by the provisions of the IBC. [9]

Legal Latin Terms Group 8

in esse - In being, existence

in forma pauperis - Permission given to a poor person to sue without liability for court costs

infra - Beneath; below

in limine - At the beginning; At the threshold

in loco parentis - In place of the parent

in pari delicto - In equal fault

in personam - Personally, or against the person

in praesenti - At once; now

in re - In the matter

in rem - A proceeding against a thing

in specie - In the same or in similar form

16

Jignesh Shah and Ors. vs. Union of India (UOI) and Ors. (25.09.2019 – SC)

Relevant Section: Companies Act, 1956 - Section 433; - Section 434; Insolvency And Bankruptcy Code, 2016 - Section 7

Hon'ble Judges/Coram: Rohinton Fali Nariman, R. Subhash Reddy and Surya Kant, JJ.

Number of PDF Pages in Original Judgement: 21

Citation: AIR2019SC4758, 2019(6)ALD200, 2020(2)ALLMR416, IV(2019)BC84(SC), [2019]152CLA519(SC), [2019]217CompCas139(SC), 2019(13)SCALE61, (2019)10SCC750, [2019]156SCL542(SC), (2020)1WBLR(SC)61, MANU/SC/1319/2019

Case Note: Insolvency - Winding up Petition - Maintainability of - Section 7 of Insolvency and Bankruptcy Code, 2016 - National Company Law Appellate Tribunal ("NCLAT") by an order dismissed appeal filed by Shri Jignesh Shah against admission order, agreeing with NCLT that transaction would fall within meaning of "financial debt" under Code, and that, bar of limitation would not be attracted as Winding up Petition was filed within three years of date on which Code came into force, viz., 1st December, 2016 - Whether Winding up Petition, on date that it was filed was barred by lapse of time.

Disposed off

Facts: Writ Petition have been filed by Shri Jignesh Shah and Smt. Pushpa Shah respectively, both of whom were shareholders of La-Fin Financial Services Pvt. Ltd. ("La-Fin") assailing order of National Company Law Tribunal, Mumbai Bench ("NCLT") admitting a winding up petition that was filed by IL & FS Financial Services Ltd. ("IL & FS") against La-Fin before High Court which was transferred to the NCLT and then heard as a Section 7 application under Insolvency and Bankruptcy Code, 2016. The National Company Law Appellate Tribunal ("NCLAT") by an order dismissed the appeal filed by Shri Jignesh Shah against the aforesaid admission order, agreeing with the NCLT that transaction would fall within the meaning of "financial debt" under the Code, and that the bar of limitation would not be attracted as the Winding up Petition was filed within three years of date on which the Code came into force, viz., 1st December, 2016. Learned Senior Advocate appearing on behalf of the Petitioners/Appellants has raised only the statutory bar of limitation against IL & FS. According to the learned Senior Advocate, after this Court's judgment in B.K. Educational Services Pvt. Ltd. v. Parag Gupta and Associates, it is clear that the Limitation Act, 1963 ("Limitation Act") would apply to all Section 7 applications that are filed under the Code and that the residuary Article, i.e., Article 137 of the Limitation Act would be attracted to the facts of this case. As the Winding up Petition that has been transferred to the NCLT was filed on 21st October, 2016, i.e., beyond the period of three years prescribed (as the cause of action had arisen in August, 2012), it is clear that a time-barred winding up petition filed under Section 433 of the Companies Act, 1956 would not suddenly get resuscitated into a Section 7 petition under the Code filed within time, by virtue of the transfer of such petition.

Hon'ble Apex Court held, while allowing the appeal

1. With the introduction of Section 238A into the Code, the provisions of the Limitation Act apply to applications made under the Code. Winding up petitions filed before the Code

came into force are now converted into petitions filed under the Code. What has, therefore, to be decided is whether the Winding up Petition, on the date that it was filed, is barred by lapse of time. If such petition is found to be time-barred, then Section 238A of the Code will not give a new lease of life to such a time-barred petition. On the facts of this case, it is clear that as the Winding up Petition was filed beyond three years from August, 2012 which is when, even according to IL & FS, default in repayment had occurred, it is barred by time. [10]

2. A suit for recovery based upon a cause of action that is within limitation cannot in any manner impact the separate and independent remedy of a winding up proceeding. In law, when time begins to run, it can only be extended in the manner provided in the Limitation Act. For example, an acknowledgement of liability under Section 18 of the Limitation Act would certainly extend the limitation period, but a suit for recovery, which is a separate and independent proceeding distinct from the remedy of winding up would, in no manner, impact the limitation within which the winding up proceeding is to be filed, by somehow keeping the debt alive for the purpose of the winding up proceeding. [19]

3. A reading of provisions would show that the starting point of the period of limitation is when the company is unable to pay its debts, and that Section 434 is a deeming provision which refers to three situations in which a Company shall be deemed to be "unable to pay its debts" under Section 433(e). In the first situation, if a demand is made by the creditor to whom the company is indebted in a sum exceeding one lakh then due, requiring the company to pay the sum so due, and the company has for three weeks thereafter "neglected to pay the sum", or to secure or compound for it to the reasonable satisfaction of the creditor. "Neglected to pay" would arise only on default to pay the sum due, which would clearly be a fixed date depending on the facts of each case. Equally in the second situation, if execution or other process is issued on a decree or order of any Court or

Tribunal in favour of a creditor of the company, and is returned unsatisfied in whole or in part, default on the part of the debtor company occurs. This again is clearly a fixed date depending on the facts of each case. And in the third situation, it is necessary to prove to the "satisfaction of the Tribunal" that the company is unable to pay its debts. Here again, the trigger point is the date on which default is committed, on account of which the Company is unable to pay its debts. This again is a fixed date that can be proved on the facts of each case. Thus, Section 433(e) read with Section 434 of the Companies Act, 1956 would show that the trigger point for the purpose of limitation for filing of a winding up petition under Section 433(e) would be the date of default in payment of the debt in any of the three situations mentioned in Section 434. [22]

4. The Bombay High Court judgment referred to in paragraph 23 of the judgment above states the law on winding up petitions filed under Section 433(a) of the Companies Act, 1956 correctly. The primary test is set out in paragraph 1, which is that a winding up petition is not a legitimate means of seeking to enforce payment of a debt which is bona fide disputed by the Company. Absent such dispute, the petition may be admitted. Equally, where the debt is bona fide disputed, there cannot be 'neglect to pay' within the meaning of Section 434(1)(a) of the Companies Act, 1956 so that the deeming provision then does not come into play. Also, the moment there is a bona fide dispute, the debt is then not 'due'. The High Court also correctly appreciates that whether the company is commercially solvent is one of the considerations in order to determine whether the company is able to pay its debts or not. [28]

5. Even on the facts of this case, the Winding up Petition alleges that the ultimatum to the Respondent company asserting that the Respondent company was legally obliged to purchase the requisite shares in accordance with the terms of the Letter of Undertaking was on 7th January, 2013. By this date at the very latest, the cause of action for filing a petition under Section

433(e) certainly arose. Also, the statutory notice given on 3rd November, 2015 does not refer to any facts as to the commercial insolvency of La-Fin. The statutory notice only refers to the suit proceedings and attachment by the EOW which had taken place long before in December 2013. [29]

6. In the Winding up Petition itself, what is referred to is the fall in the assets of La-Fin to being worth approximately INR 200 crores as of October, 2016, which again does not correlate with 3rd November, 2015, being the date on which the statutory notice was itself issued. This again is only for the purpose of appointing an Officer of the Court as Official Liquidator in order to manage the day-to-day affairs and otherwise secure and safeguard the assets of the Respondent company. There is no averment in the petition that thanks to these or other facts the Company's substratum has disappeared, or that the Company is otherwise commercially insolvent. It is clear therefore that even on facts, the company's substratum disappearing or the commercial insolvency of the company has not been pleaded. Whereas, in Form-1, upon transfer of the winding up proceedings to the NCLT, what is correctly stated is that the date of default is 19th August, 2012; making it clear that three-years from that date had long since elapsed when the Winding up Petition Under Section 433(e) was filed on 21st October, 2016. [30]

7. Present Court allows Civil Appeal and dispose of the Writ Petition by holding that, the Winding up Petition filed on 21st October, 2016 being beyond the period of three-years mentioned in Article 137 of the Limitation Act is time-barred, and cannot therefore be proceeded with any further. Accordingly, the impugned judgment of the NCLAT and the judgment of the NCLT is set aside. [31]

17

RAJENDRA K. BHUTTA VS. MAHARASHTRA HOUSING AND AREA DEVELOPMENT AUTHORITY AND ORS. (19.02.2020 – SC)

Relevant Section: Insolvency And Bankruptcy Code, 2016 - Section 14(1)(d)

Hon'ble Judges/Coram: Rohinton Fali Nariman, S. Ravindra Bhat and V. Ramasubramanian, JJ.

Number of PDF Pages in Original Judgement: 21

Citation: 2020(4)CTC692, [2020]160SCL95(SC), MANU/SC/0226/2020

Case Note: Company - Physical occupation - Recovery of property - Sections 14, 14(1)(d), 18, 31(3), 36 and 238 of Insolvency and Bankruptcy Code, 2016 - Resolution was passed by Development Authority to execute joint development agreement with Corporate Debtor - Tripartite Joint Development Agreement was entered into between Society representing persons occupying tenements, Development Authority and Corporate Debtor - Loan Agreement was entered into and executed between bank and Corporate Debtor - As result of Corporate Debtor defaulting in repayment of loan to its financial creditor, Insolvency Application under Section 7 of Code, was admitted appointing Interim Resolution Professional (Appellant) - Moratorium in terms of Section 14 was also declared by this order - After imposition of moratorium, Authority issued termination notice to Corporate Debtor of termination of Joint Development Agreement - It was further stated that Corporate Debtor would have to handover possession to Development Authority, which would then enter upon plot and take possession of land including all structures thereon - Appellant filed application seeking direction from Tribunal to restrain Development Authority from taking over possession of land till completion of CIRP - Tribunal dismissed application, stating that Section 14(1)(d) of Code did not cover licenses to enter upon land in pursuance of Joint Development Agreements - Appeal against this order was preferred to Appellate Tribunal - Appellate Tribunal held that land could not be treated to be asset of Corporate Debtor for application of provisions of Section 14(1)(d) of Code - Hence, present appeal - Whether Appellate Tribunal erred in holding that land could not be treated to be asset of Corporate Debtor for application of provisions of Section 14(1)(d) of Code.

Appeal Allowed

Facts: A Resolution was passed by the Development Authority to execute a joint development agreement with the Corporate Debtor. The State Government granted its approval to the aforesaid Resolution. A Tripartite Joint Development Agreement was entered into between the Society representing persons occupying tenements, Development Authority and the Corporate Debtor. A Loan Agreement was entered into and executed between the bank and the Corporate Debtor for a sum. As a result of the Corporate Debtor defaulting in repayment of the loan to its financial creditor, an Insolvency Application under Section 7 of the Code, was admitted appointing an Interim Resolution Professional. A moratorium in terms of Section 14 was also declared by this order. After the imposition of the moratorium period under Section 14 of the Code, Development Authority issued a termination notice to the Corporate Debtor stating that upon expiry of thirty days from the date of receipt of the notice, the Joint Development Agreement as modified would stand terminated. It was further stated that the Corporate Debtor would have to handover possession to Development Authority, which would then enter upon the plot and take possession of the land including all structures thereon. The Appellant filed application seeking a direction from the Tribunal to restrain Development Authority from taking over possession of the land till completion of the CIRP, contending that such a recovery of possession was in derogation of the moratorium imposed under Section 14 of the Code. The Tribunal dismissed the application, stating that Section 14(1)(d) of the Code did not cover licenses to enter upon land in pursuance of Joint Development Agreements, stating that such licenses would only be personal and not interests created in property. An appeal against this order was preferred to the NCLAT. The Appellate Tribunal held that land could not be treated to be the asset of the Corporate Debtor for application of provisions of Section 14(1)(d) of the Code.

Hon'ble Apex Court held, while allowing the appeal:

i. A bare reading of Section 14(1)(d) of the Code would make it clear that it does not deal with any of the assets or legal right or beneficial interest in such assets of the corporate debtor. For this reason, any reference to Sections 18 and 36, as was made by the NCLT, becomes wholly unnecessary in deciding the scope of Section 14(1)(d), which stands on a separate footing. Under Section 14(1)(d) what was referred to was the recovery of any property. The property in this case consists of land, together with structures thereon that had to be demolished. Recovery would necessarily go with what was parted by the corporate debtor, and for this one had to go to the next expression contained in the said Sub-section. [7]

ii. The expression occupied by would mean or be synonymous with being in actual physical possession of or being actually used by, in contra-distinction to the expression possession, which would connote possession being either constructive or actual and which, in turn, would include legally being in possession, though factually not being in physical possession. Since it was clear that the Joint Development Agreement read with the Deed of Modification has granted a license to the developer (Corporate Debtor) to enter upon the property, with a view to do all the things that were mentioned in it, there could be no gain saying that after such entry, the property would be occupied by the developer. [15]

iii. There was no doubt whatsoever that important functions relating to repairs and re-construction of dilapidated buildings are given to MHADA. Equally, there was no doubt that in a given set of circumstances, the Board may, on such terms and conditions as may be agreed upon, and with the previous approval of the Authority, handover execution of any housing scheme under its own supervision. However, when it comes to any clash between the MHADA Act and the Insolvency Code, on the plain terms of Section 238 of the Insolvency Code, the Code must prevail. This is for the very good reason that when a moratorium was spoken of by Section 14 of the Code, the idea was that, to alleviate corporate sickness, a statutory status quo was pronounced under Section 14 the moment a petition was admitted under Section 7 of the Code, so that the insolvency resolution process may proceed unhindered by any of the obstacles that would otherwise be caused and that were dealt with by Section 14. The statutory freeze that had thus been made was, unlike its predecessor in the SICA, 1985 only a limited one, which was expressly limited by Section 31(3) of the Code, to the date of admission of an insolvency petition up to the date that the Adjudicating Authority either allows a resolution plan to come into effect or states that the corporate debtor must go into the liquidation. For this temporary period, at least, all the things referred to under Section 14 must be strictly observed so that the corporate debtor may finally be put back on its feet albeit with a new management. [16]

18

RAHUL JAIN VS. RAVE SCANS PVT. LTD. AND ORS. (08.11.2019 – SC)

Relevant Section: Insolvency And Bankruptcy Code, 2016 - Section 30

Hon'ble Judges/Coram: Arun Mishra and S. Ravindra Bhat, JJ.

Number of PDF Pages in Original Judgement: 6

Citation: 2020 (139) ALR 713, [2019]153CLA152(SC), 2019(15) SCALE528, (2019)10SCC548, [2020]157SCL531(SC), MANU/SC/1537/2019

Case Note: Company - Resolution plan - Modification of - Section 10 of Insolvency and Bankruptcy Code, 2016 - Corporate Insolvency Resolution Process (CIRP) was initiated against Corporate Debtor under Section 10 of Code - Revised resolution plan submitted by Appellant was approved by National Company Law Tribunal (NCLT) - Second Respondent-Financial Creditor appealed against NCLT's order on grounds of discrimination between financial creditors, which resulted in NCLAT modifying the NCLT's final order - Hence, present appeal - Whether finding that financial creditor was discriminated against, leading NCLAT to modify adjudicating authority's directions, and consequently imposing greater financial burdens on resolution applicant, was justified.

Appeal Allowed

Facts: The Corporate Insolvency Resolution Process (CIRP) was initiated against the Corporate Debtor under Section 10 of the Insolvency and Bankruptcy Code, 2016. The revised resolution plan submitted by the Appellant was approved by the NCLT. The second Respondent-Financial Creditor appealed against the NCLT's order on grounds of discrimination between financial creditors, which resulted in the NCLAT modifying the NCLT's final order.

Hon'ble Apex Court held, while allowing the appeal:

It was noticeable that no doubt, second Respondent was provided with certain percentage of its admitted claim as it had dissented with the plan. On the other hand, other company was provided with certain percentage of its admitted claim, other financial creditors were provided with forty five percent of their admitted claims. Given that the resolution process began well before the amended Regulation came into force and the resolution plan was prepared and approved before that event, the wide observations of the NCLAT, requiring the Appellant to match the pay-out to second Respondent, was not justified. The court notices that the liquidation value of the corporate debtor was ascertained at thirty six crores. Against the said amount, the Appellant offered fifty four crore rupees. The plan was approved and, except the objections of the dissenting creditor, the plan had attained finality. Having regard to these factors and circumstances, it was held that the NCLAT's order and directions were not justified. They were hereby set aside and the order of the NCLT was hereby restored. [13]

19

B. K. EDUCATIONAL SERVICES PRIVATE LIMITED VS. PARAG GUPTA AND ASSOCIATES (11.10.2018 – SC)

Relevant Section: Sections 7 and 9 of Insolvency and Bankruptcy Code, 2016 & Limitation Act

Hon'ble Judges/Coram: Rohinton Fali Nariman and Navin Sinha, JJ.

Number of PDF Pages in Original Judgement: 25

Citations : AIR2018SC5601, 2019(1)ALD136, IV(2018)BC317(SC), [2018]146CLA380(SC), [2019]212CompCas1(SC), (2018)4CompLJ209(SC), 2018(6)CTC438, 2019-2-LW939, 2018(14)SCALE482, (2019)11SCC633, 2018 (10) SCJ 407, [2018]150SCL293(SC), MANU/SC/1160/2018)

Case Note: Company - Applicability of act - Sections 7 and 9 of Insolvency and Bankruptcy Code, 2016 - Appellate Authority had held that Limitation Act, 1963 was not applicable for initiation of Corporate Insolvency Resolution Process and Doctrine of Limitation and Prescription was necessary to be looked into for determining question whether application under Section 7 or Section 9 could be entertained after long delay, amounting to laches and thereby person forfeited his claim - Hence, present appeal - Whether Limitation

Act, 1963 would apply to applications that were made under Section 7 or Section 9 of Code on and from its commencement. –

Appeal Disposed Off

Facts: The Appellate Authority held that the Limitation Act, 1963 was not applicable for initiation of Corporate Insolvency Resolution Process and further hold that the Doctrine of Limitation and Prescription was necessary to be looked into for determining the question whether the application under Section 7 or Section 9 of Act could be entertained after long delay, amounting to laches and thereby the person forfeited his claim.

Hon'ble Apex Court held, while disposing off the appeal:

1. It may also be noticed that Under Section 434(1)(c) of the Companies Act, all proceedings under the Companies Act, including the proceedings relating to winding up of companies, pending immediately before such date, before any District Court or High Court, shall stand transferred to the Tribunal and the Tribunal may proceed to deal with such proceedings from the stage before they are transferred. This Section is also important in that it indicates that proceedings under the Companies Act relating to arbitration, compromise, arrangements and reconstruction and winding up of companies, that were pending before the District Court or the High Court, may now be transferred to the Tribunal. Each of these proceedings would directly be governed by the Limitation Act as they are proceedings before Courts. Obviously, upon transfer of such proceedings to the Tribunal, it cannot be stated that because these proceedings are now before the Tribunal, the Limitation Act will cease to apply. Also, in fresh applications that are made after the Code comes into force, it cannot be said that to such applications, the Limitation Act will not apply, but to applications that are transferred from the District Court or the High Court, the provisions of the Limitation Act will apply. In particular, winding up proceedings pending before a High Court are liable to be transferred to the

NCLT for further decision by applying the Code and not the Companies Act. [8]

2. It was thus clear that Section 433 of the Companies Act, 2013 would apply to the Tribunal even when it decides applications under Sections 7 and 9 of the Code. [9]

3. Insofar as the Code was concerned, the intention of the legislature, from the very beginning, was to apply the Limitation Act to the NCLT and the NCLAT while deciding applications filed under Sections 7 and 9 of the Code and appeals therefrom. Section 433 of the Companies Act, which applies to the Tribunal and the Appellate Tribunal, expressly applies the Limitation Act to the Appellate Tribunal, the NCLAT, as well. Also, the argument that the NCLAT was an appellate tribunal which is common to three statutes, under one of which, viz., the Competition Act, no period of limitation had been prescribed, would not lead to any anomalous situation. When the Appellate Tribunal, i.e., the NCLAT decides an appeal under the Competition Act, since an appeal is a continuation of the application filed before the Competition Commission, the NCLAT would decide the appeal on the footing that the Limitation Act did not apply to an application made before the Competition Commission. On the other hand, insofar as applications were filed under Section 7 or 9 of the Code, or petitions or applications filed under the Companies Act, the NCLAT would decide such petitions/applications on the footing that the Limitation Act would apply to such petitions/applications. Merely because appeals under different statutes were sent to one appellate tribunal would make no difference to the position in law. Undoubtedly, if three separate appellate tribunals had been constituted under the three enactments in question, this argument would have no legs to stand on. Merely because, from the point of view of convenience, appeals were filed before one appellate forum would not mean that any anomalous situation would arise as each appeal would be decided keeping in mind the provisions of the particular Act in question. [25]

4. It was thus clear that since the Limitation Act is applicable to applications filed under Sections 7 and 9 of the Code from the inception of the Code, Article 137 of the Limitation Act gets attracted. The right to sue, therefore, accrues when a default occurs. If the default has occurred over three years prior to the date of filing of the application, the application would be barred under Article 137 of the Limitation Act, save and except in those cases where, in the facts of the case, Section 5 of the Limitation Act may be applied to condone the delay in filing such application. [27]

Legal Latin Terms Group 9

instanter - Immediately

inter alia, inter alios - Among other things or between other persons

inter se - Among themselves

inter vivos - Between the living; or from one person to another

in toto - In the whole; completely

in transitu - In transit

intra - Within; inside

ipse dixit - He himself said (it), as an assertion made but not proved

ipso facto - By the fact itself

ita est - so it is

jura personarum - Right of a person, rights of persons

20

STATE BANK OF INDIA VS. V. RAMAKRISHNAN AND ORS. (14.08.2018 – SC)

Relevant Section: Sections 14, 60(2),96 and 101 of Insolvency and Bankruptcy Code, 2016

Hon'ble Judges/Coram: Rohinton Fali Nariman and Indu Malhotra, JJ.

Number of PDF Pages in Original Judgement: 21

Citations : 2018(6)ABR42, AIR2018SC3876, 2018(5)ALD162, III(2018)BC593(SC), 2018(6)BomCR47, [2018]145CLA447(SC), [2018]210CompCas364(SC), (2018)4CompLJ48(SC), 2019(1)CTC889,2018(5)MhLj692,2018(4)MPLJ23,2018(4)RCR(Civil)110, 2018(9)SCALE597, 2018 (7) SCJ 632, [2018]149SCL107(SC)/ MANU/SC/0849/2018

Case Note: Banking - Personal guarantor - Applicability of provision - Sections 14,60(2),96 and 101 of Insolvency and Bankruptcy Code, 2016 - Respondent No. 1 was personal guarantor in respect of credit facilities availed by Respondent No. 2 - Respondent No. 2 Company did not pay its debts and application to initiate corporate insolvency resolution process against itself, was admitted - Application was filed by Respondent No. 1 as personal guarantor, with plea that Section 14 of Code would apply to personal guarantor as well - Tribunal allowed application which was confirmed by Appellate Tribunal - Hence, present appeal - Whether Section 14 of Code, would apply to personal guarantor of corporate debtor. –

Appeals allowed.

Facts: Respondent No. 1 was the Managing Director of the corporate debtor, namely, the Respondent No. 2 Company, and also the personal guarantor in respect of credit facilities that had been availed from the Appellant. Respondent No. 2 Company did not pay its debts in time. An application was filed by Respondent No. 2, the corporate debtor, under Section 10 of the Code to initiate the corporate insolvency resolution process against itself, which was admitted. Application was filed by Respondent No. 1 as personal guarantor to the corporate debtor, in which Respondent No. 1 took up the plea that Section 14 of the Code would apply to the personal guarantor as well. Tribunal, held that since under Section 31 of the Code, a Resolution Plan made thereunder would bind the personal guarantor as well, and since, after the creditor is proceeded against, the guarantor stands in the shoes of the creditor, Section 14 would apply in favour of the personal guarantor as well. An appeal filed to the National Company Law Appellate Tribunal resulted in the appeal being dismissed.

Hon'ble Apex Court held, while allowing the appeal:

1. Sub-section (2) of Section 60 of Code speaks of an application relating to the bankruptcy of a personal guarantor of a corporate debtor and states that any such bankruptcy proceedings shall be filed only before the National Company Law Tribunal. The argument of the Respondents that bankruptcy would include SARFAESI proceedings must be turned down as bankruptcy had reference only to the two Insolvency Acts. Thus, SARFAESI proceedings against the guarantor could continue under the SARFAESI Act. Similarly, Sub-section (3) speaks of a bankruptcy proceeding of a personal guarantor of the corporate debtor pending in any Court or Tribunal, which shall

stand transferred to the Adjudicating Authority dealing with the insolvency resolution process or liquidation proceedings of such corporate debtor. An Adjudicating Authority, defined under Section 5(1) of the Code, means the National Company Law Tribunal constituted under the Companies Act, 2013. [20]

2. Sections 96 and 101 of Code, when contrasted with Section 14 of Code, would show that Section 14 of Code could not possibly apply to a personal guarantor. When an application was filed under Part III, an interim-moratorium or a moratorium was applicable in respect of any debt due. First and foremost, this was a separate moratorium, applicable separately in the case of personal guarantors against whom insolvency resolution processes may be initiated under Part III. Secondly, the protection of the moratorium under these Sections was far greater than that of Section 14 of Code in that pending legal proceedings in respect of the debt and not the debtor are stayed. The difference in language between Sections 14 and 101 of Code was for a reason. Section 14 of Code refers only to debts due by corporate debtors, who are limited liability companies, and it was clear that in the vast majority of cases, personal guarantees are given by Directors who are in management of the companies. The object of the Code was not to allow such guarantors to escape from an independent and co-extensive liability to pay off the entire outstanding debt, which was why Section 14 of Code was not applied to them. [23]

21

TRANSMISSION CORPORATION OF ANDHRA PRADESH LIMITED VS. EQUIPMENT CONDUCTORS AND CABLES LIMITED (23.10.2018 – SC)

Relevant Section: Section 9 of Insolvency and Bankruptcy Code, 2016

Hon'ble Judges/Coram: A.K. Sikri and Ashok Bhushan, JJ.

Number of PDF Pages in Original Judgement: 11

Citation: I(2019)BC52(SC), 2019(1) CHN (SC) 117, [2018]147CLA112(SC), (2019)1CompLJ74(SC), 2018(14) SCALE176, (2019)12SCC697, [2018]150SCL447(SC), MANU/SC/1192/2018

Case Note: Company - Settlement of claim - Direction - Challenge thereto - Section 9 of the Insolvency and Bankruptcy Code, 2016 (IBC) - Order of National Company Law Appellate Tribunal was subject matter of challenge in present proceedings - Whether Appellant was liable to settle purported claim.

Appeal Allowed

Facts: Appellant was a Transmission Corporation of Andhra Pradesh Government and was in activities relating to transmission of electricity. It had awarded certain contracts to Respondent for supply of goods and services. Some disputes arose and Respondent initiated arbitration proceedings. 82 claims were filed by Respondent before Haryana Micro and Small Enterprises Facilitation Council ('Arbitral Council') which concluded that, claims made on basis of Invoice Nos. 1-57 were barred by law of limitation and, therefore, no amount could be awarded against said claims. In respect of Invoice Nos. 58-82, award was passed in favour of Respondent. NCLT also dismissed petition. In instant matter, NCLAT perceived that, Appellant owed money to Respondent and for this reason, a chance was given to Appellant to settle claim of Respondent, otherwise order would be passed initiating Corporate Insolvency Resolution Process ('CIRP'). According to Appellant, no amount was payable and the order in question was causing serious prejudice to Appellant which was asked to settle the purported claim, failing which, to face insolvency proceedings.

Hon'ble Apex Court held, while allowing the appeals

1. Existence of an undisputed debt is sine qua non of initiating CIRP. It also followed that, adjudicating authority shall satisfy itself that, there was a debt payable and there was operational debt and corporate debtor had not repaid the same. [10]

2. Matter was taken up before Arbitral Council insofar as claim under Invoice Nos. 1-53 was concerned, same was specifically rejected by Arbitral Council on ground that, it had become time barred. Respondent challenged said part of award of Arbitral Council, but was not successful. On basis of certain observations made by High Court, Respondent attempted to recover amount by filing execution petition before Civil Court. However, that attempt of Respondent was also unsuccessful as High Court held that, since that particular amount was not payable under award, execution was not maintainable. After failing to recover amount in aforesaid manner, Respondent issued notice to Appellant under Section 8 of IBC treating itself as operational creditor and Appellant as corporate debtor. Appellant specifically refuted

this claim. In spite thereof, application under Section 9 was filed before NCLT, Hyderabad which was dismissed by it vide order. [12]

3. NCLAT had notdiscussed merits of case and also not stated how amount was payable to Respondent in spite of aforesaid events which were noted by NCLT as well. Notwithstanding, it had given wielded threat to Appellant by giving a one chance, 'to settle claim with Appellant (Respondent herein), failing which present Appellate Tribunal might pass appropriate orders on merit'. There was a clear message in aforesaid order directing Appellant to pay amount to Respondent, failing which CIRP shall be initiated against Appellant. [13]

4. As of today, there was no award of Arbitral Council with respect to invoices at Sl. Nos. 1-57. There was no order of any other Court as well qua these invoices. In fact, Arbitral Council specifically rejected claim of Respondent as time barred. [14]

5. In a recent judgment of this Court in Mobilox Innovations Private Limited v. Kirusa Software Private Limited, this Court had categorically laid down that, IBC was not intended to be substitute to a recovery forum. It was also laid down that, whenever there was existence of real dispute, IBC provisions could not be invoked. [15]

6. Impugned order dated September 04, 2018 passed by NCLAT was set aside. Appeal allowed [15]

22

RELIANCE COMMUNICATION LIMITED AND ORS. VS. STATE BANK OF INDIA AND ORS. (20.02.2019 – SC)

Relevant Section: Contempt Of Courts Act, 1971 - Section 12(4), Insolvency and Bankruptcy Code, 2016 - Section 9; Constitution of India - Article 142

Hon'ble Judges/Coram: Rohinton Fali Nariman and Vineet Saran, JJ.

Number of PDF Pages in Original Judgement: 19

Citation: AIR2019SC1196, 2019(4)ALD58, 2019(2)ALT60, [2019]151CLA11(SC), (2019)2CompLJ401(SC), 2019(3) SCALE428, 2019 (4) SCJ 416 I, MANU/SC/0250/2019

Case Note: Contempt of Court - Disobedience of order - Petitioner and Respondents entered into Managed Service Agreement whereby Petitioner agreed to provide Respondent managed services - Petitioner raised invoices from time to time in consideration of services provided, and on receiving no payment -Company Tribunal appointed Interim Resolution Professionals to carry out corporate insolvency resolution process - Appeals were filed against in Appellate Tribunal, who stayed orders and recorded statement of Respondent that amount would be paid within one hundred twenty days time - Respondent filed writ petition in this Court for closure of corporate insolvency resolution process - This Court recorded that timeline of one hundred twenty days shall be strictly adhered to - Respondent applied for extension of time for payment by sixty days, and this court made clear, as last opportunity, amount must be paid - Second application to extend time was moved, citing excuse of other spectrum not yet being saleable, which was dismissed as withdrawn - Hence, present petition - Whether there was any disobedience of order passed by this Court by Respondent companies.

Disposed off

Facts: Petitioner and Respondent companies entered into a Managed Service Agreement whereby Petitioner agreed to provide Respondent managed services, i.e., operation, maintenance, and management of network. Petitioner raised invoices from time to time in consideration of services provided, and on receiving no payment, ultimately issued three notices, under the Insolvency and Bankruptcy Code, 2016. Petitioner filed applications under Section 9 of the Code as operational creditors. The National Company Law Tribunal admitted the said petitions and appointed three Interim Resolution Professionals to carry out the corporate insolvency resolution process. Appeals were filed in Appellate Tribunal who, stayed the orders and recorded the statement that the matter had been agreed to be settled for a sum, which would be paid within one hundred twenty days' time. Respondent Companies filed a writ petition in this Court in which they asked for quashing/closure of the corporate insolvency resolution process in view of settlement of disputes between them and Petitioner. This Court recorded that the timeline of one hundred twenty days shall be strictly adhered to and payment was to be made. Respondent applied for extension of time for payment by sixty days, and this court made clear, as last opportunity, amount must be paid. The Second application to extend time was moved, citing excuse of other spectrum not yet being saleable. This Court made it clear that it was not inclined to grant any such extension, as a result of which, the second application for extension of time was dismissed as withdrawn.

Hon'ble Apex Court held, while disposing off the petition:

1. The undertakings given by the Chairmen of the Respondent companies were neither as per the Court's understanding of its order, nor the understanding of the three Companies themselves, as was clear from the undertakings given by the three Directors pursuant to the order. It was clear that the Respondent-Companies had no intention, at the very least, of adhering to the time limit of one hundred twenty days or to the extended time limit of sixty days plus, as was given by way of indulgence. The undertakings given on the footing that the amount would be paid only out of the sale of assets was false to the knowledge of the Petitioner Companies. This itself affects the administration of justice, and was therefore, contempt of court. [17]

2. The contempt of this Court needs to be purged by payment of the sum together with interest till date. As stated by the letter, subject to any calculation error, an amount must be paid to Petitioner in addition to the deposit of amount made in the Registry of this Court. The Registry of this Court was directed to pay over the sum to Petitioner within a period of one week from today. The Respondent was directed to purge the contempt of this Court by payment to Petitioner within a period of four weeks from today. In default of such payment, the Chairmen who have given undertakings to this Court will suffer three months' imprisonment. [24]

23

Jaipur Metals and Electricals Employees Organization vs. Jaipur Metals and Electricals Ltd. and Ors. (12.12.2018 – SC)

Relevant Section: Sick Industrial Companies (Special Provisions) Act, 1985 [Repealed] - Section 20; Companies Act, 2013 - Section 419(4), Section 434, Section 434(1); Section 10E(1), Insolvency and Bankruptcy Code, 2016 - Section 7, Section 8, Section 9, Section 14, Section 238, Section 239, Section 255

Hon'ble Judges/Coram: Rohinton Fali Nariman and M.R. Shah, JJ.

Number of PDF Pages in Original Judgement: 11

Citation: 2019 (133) ALR 269, 2019(1)BomCR801, 2019(2) CHN (SC) 42, [2019]148CLA143(SC), [2019]213CompCas25(SC), 2019(1)CTC587, 2019(1)RCR(Civil)358, 2019 143 RD590, 2018(15)SCALE836, (2019)4SCC227, 2019 (5) SCJ 249, [2019]151SCL196(SC), (2019)4WBLR(SC)116, 2019 (1) WLN 131 (SC), MANU/SC/1466/2018

Case Note: Company - Winding up proceedings - Transfer - Present appeal had been filed by an employees' union challenging judgment of High Court in which High Court had refused to transfer winding up proceedings pending before it to National Company Law Tribunal ("NCLT"), and had set aside an order of NCLT by which order, a financial creditor's petition under Section 7 of Insolvency and Bankruptcy Code, 2016 ("Insolvency Code" or "Code") had been admitted.

Appeal Allowed

Facts: On 30th September, 1997, account of Respondent No. 1 company had become a non-performing asset, and since company's net worth had turned negative, a reference was made to Board for Industrial and Financial Reconstruction ("BIFR") under Sick Industrial Companies (Special Provisions) Act, 1985 ("SIC Act"). On 26th September, 2002, BIFR was of prima facie opinion that company ought to be wound up, which opinion was forwarded to High Court. High Court ultimately registered case as Company Petition No. 19/2009. Alchemist Asset Reconstruction Company Ltd. (Respondent No. 3) acquired substantially all financial debts of Respondent No. 1. State of Rajasthan tried to revive company, but with no success. Ultimately, in a writ petition filed by a workers' union, being Writ Petition No. 504/2000, High Court, on 07.12.2017, directed Official Liquidator to be provisionally attached to Court, and to join in evaluation of value of goods and material lying in factory premises of company so that dues of workmen could be paid. In meanwhile, on 11.01.2018, Respondent No. 3 herein preferred an application Under Section 7 of Insolvency Code, stating that it had an assigned debt of INR 356 crores owed to it by Respondent No. 1. Considering fact that debt was admitted by company and that till date no liquidation order had been passed in winding up proceedings that were pending before High Court, NCLT held, referring to non-obstante Clause contained in Section 238 of Insolvency Code, that it was satisfied that conditions of Section 7 had been fulfilled and that, refore, application should be admitted. Accordingly, a moratorium was declared in terms of Section 14 of Code and an interim resolution professional was appointed.

Hon'ble Apex Court held, while allowing the appeal

1. Under Section 434 as substituted by Eleventh Schedule to Code vide notification dated 15th November, 2016, all proceedings under Companies Act, 2013 which relate to winding up of

companies and which were pending immediately before such date as may be notified by Central Government in this behalf shall stand transferred to NCLT. Stage at which such proceedings were to be transferred to NCLT was such as might be prescribed by Central Government. [12]

2. When Rules 5 and 6 of 2016 Transfer Rules (un-amended) were read, it was clear that three types of proceedings were referred to. Under Rule 5(1), petitions which relate to winding up under Clause (e) of Section 433 of Companies Act, 1956 on ground of inability to pay debts that were pending before High Court were to be transferred to NCLT in case petition had not been served on Respondent. They shall then be treated as applications Uunder Sections 7, 8, or 9 of Code and dealt with in accordance with Part II of Code. Similarly, all petitions filed under Clauses (a) and (f) of Section 433 of Companies Act, 1956 pending before High Court, in which petition had not been served on Respondents, shall be transferred to NCLT. Only such petitions will continue to be treated as petitions under provisions of Companies Act, 2013. third category of cases dealt with by Rules 5 and 6 was contained in Rule 5(2). This category related to cases where BIFR had forwarded an opinion to High Court to wind up a company Under Section 20 of SIC Act. All such cases, whatever be stage, shall continue to be dealt with by High Court in accordance with provisions of SIC Act. [13]

3. It was clear that present case related to Rule 5(2) alone. Despite fact that, Section 20 of SIC Act spoke of a company being wound up under Companies Act, 1956 under just and equitable provision, which was Section 433(f) of Companies Act, 1956, yet, since cases that fall under Section 20 of SIC Act were dealt with separately under Rule 5(2), they could not be treated as petitions that had been filed under Section 433(f) of Companies Act, 1956, which were separately specified under Rule 6. High Court was therefore not correct in treating petitions that were pursuant to Section 20 of SIC Act as being pursuant to Section 433(f) of Companies Act, 1956 and applying Rule 6 of 2016 Transfer Rules. [14]

4. Effect of omission of Rule 5(2) was not to automatically transfer all cases under Section 20 of SIC Act to NCLT, as otherwise, a specific Rule would have to be framed transferring such cases to NCLT, as had been done in Rule 5(1). real reason for omission of Rule 5(2) in substituted Rule 5 was because it was necessary to state, only once, on repeal of SIC Act, that proceedings under Section 20 of SIC Act shall continue to be dealt with by High Court. It was unnecessary to continue Rule 5(2) even after 29.06.2017 as on 15.12.2016, all pending cases under Section 20 of SIC Act were to continue to be dealt with by High Court before which such cases were pending. Since, there could be no opinion by BIFR under Section 20 of SIC Act after 01.12.2016, when SIC Act was repealed, it was unnecessary to continue Rule 5(2) as, on 15.12.2016, all pending proceedings under Section 20 of SIC Act were to continue with High Court and would continue even thereafter. This was further made clear by amendment to Section 434(1)(c), with effect from 17th August, 2018, where any party to a winding up proceeding pending before a Court immediately before this date may file an application for transfer of such proceedings, and Court, at that stage, may, by order, transfer such proceedings to NCLT. Proceedings so transferred would then be dealt with by NCLT as an application for initiation of corporate insolvency resolution process under Code. It was thus clear that, under scheme of Section 434 (as amended) and Rule 5 of 2016 Transfer Rules, all proceedings under Section 20 of SIC Act pending before High Court were to continue as such until a party files an application before High Court for transfer of such proceedings post 17.08.2018. Once this was done, High Court must transfer such proceedings to NCLT which would then deal with such proceedings as an application for initiation of corporate insolvency resolution process under Code. [15]

5. Respondent No. 3 had filed a Section 7 application under Code on 11.01.2018, on which an order had been passed admitting such application by NCLT on 13.04.2018. This proceeding was an independent proceeding which had nothing to do with transfer of pending winding up proceedings before High Court.

It was open for Respondent No. 3 at any time before a winding up order was passed to apply under Section 7 of Code. [17]

6. NCLT was absolutely correct in applying Section 238 of Code to an independent proceeding instituted by a secured financial creditor, namely, Alchemist Asset Reconstruction Company Ltd. This being case, it was difficult to comprehend how High Court could had held that proceedings before NCLT were without jurisdiction. On this score, refore, High Court judgment had to be set aside. NCLT proceedings would now continue from stage at which y had been left off. Company petition pending before High Court could not be proceeded with further in view of Section 238 of Code. Writ petitions that were pending before High Court had also to be disposed of in light of fact that proceedings under Code must run their entire course. High Court's judgment was set aside. Appeal allowed [18]

Legal Latin Terms Group 10

jura rerum - Rights of things

jure divino - By divine rights

jure uxoris - In his wife's right

jus - Law or right

jus ad rem - A right to a thing

jus commune - The common law or common right

jus gentium - The law of nations or international law

just habendi - The right to have a thing and retain the profits

jus tertii - The right of a third party

levari facias - Cause to be levied, a writ of execution

lex – Law

24

FORECH INDIA LTD. VS. EDELWEISS ASSETS RECONSTRUCTION CO. LTD. (22.01.2019 – SC)

Relevant Section: Sick Industrial Companies (Special Provisions) Act, 1985 [Repealed] - Section 20; Companies Act, 2013 - Section 419(4), Section 434, Section 434(1); Insolvency and Bankruptcy Code, 2016 - Section 9; Section 10

Hon'ble Judges/Coram: Rohinton Fali Nariman and Navin Sinha, JJ

Number of PDF Pages in Original Judgement: 11

Citation: : I(2019)BC521(SC), [2019]148CLA409(SC), [2019]213CompCas121(SC), 2019(2)RCR(Civil)77, 2019(2)SCALE142, 2019 (2) SCJ 505, [2019]152SCL145(SC), MANU/SC/0080/2019

Case Note: Company - Winding up proceedings - Continuity thereto - Section 9, 10 of Insolvency & Bankruptcy Code, 2016; Rule 26, 27 of Companies (Court) Rules - Present matter arose from an Operational Creditor's appeal to continue with a winding up petition that had been filed by said creditor way back in 2014 - Whether winding up proceedings before High Court should continue and not proceedings filed by other creditors under the Code.

Disposed off

Facts: A winding up petition, was filed by present Appellant before High Court against Respondent No. 2-Company, alleging (Under Section 433(e) of companies Act) inability to pay dues. Notice in present petition had been served, as was recorded by an order of High Court. It was also pointed out by learned Counsel for Appellant that, a Reference had been made by Company itself on 14.07.2015 to Board for Industrial and Financial Reconstruction (BIFR) under Sick Industrial Companies Act, 1985, which, according to Appellant, had abated as on 11th December, 2016. It transpired that, another operational creditor, viz., SKF India Ltd. had filed an application under Section 9 of Insolvency & Bankruptcy Code, 2016, against Respondent No. 2, which was allowed to be withdrawn so that aforesaid operational creditor could go to High Court in a winding up petition which would then be heard along with Company Petition. Meanwhile, Respondent No. 1, being a financial creditor of selfsame corporate debtor, moved National Company Law Tribunal (NCLT) in an insolvency petition filed under Section 7 of Code sometime in May/June 2017. This petition was admitted. Against aforesaid order, an appeal was filed by Appellant herein which was dismissed by Appellate Tribunal, in which Section 11 of Code was referred to, and it was held by Appellate Tribunal that, since there was no winding up order by High Court, financial creditor's petition would be maintainable, as a result of which Appellant's appeal had been dismissed.

Hon'ble Apex Court held, while disposing off the appeal:

1. Rules 26 and 27 clearly referred to a pre-admission scenario as was clear from a plain reading of Rules 26 and 27, which made it clear that, notice contained in Form No. 6 had to be served in not less than 14 days before date of hearing. Hence, expression "was admitted" in Form No. 6 only meant that, notice had been issued in winding up petition which was then "fixed for hearing before Company Judge" on a certain day. Thus, Madras High

Court view was plainly incorrect whereas Bombay High Court view is correct in law. [16]

2. When Code was enacted, only winding up petitions, where no notice under Rule 26 of Companies (Court) Rules was served, were to be transferred to NCLT and treated as petitions under Code. However, on a working of Code, Government realized that parallel proceedings in High Courts as well as before adjudicating authority in Code would stultify objective sought to be achieved by Code, which was to resuscitate corporate debtors who were in red. In accordance with this objective, Rules kept being amended, until finally Section 434 was itself substituted in 2018, in which a proviso was added by which even in winding up petitions where notice had been served and which were pending in High Courts, any person could apply for transfer of such petitions to the NCLT under the Code, which would then had to be transferred by High Court to adjudicating authority and treated as an insolvency petition under the Code. [17]

3. Section 11 of Code was of limited application and only barred a corporate debtor from initiating a petition under Section 10 of Code in respect of whom a liquidation order had been made. From a reading of this Section, it did not follow that until a liquidation order had been made against corporate debtor, an Insolvency Petition might be filed under Section 7 or Section 9 as case might be, as had been held by Appellate Tribunal. Hence, any reference to Section 11 in context of the problem was wholly irrelevant. However, present Court declined to interfere with ultimate order passed by Appellate Tribunal because it was clear that, financial creditor's application which had been admitted by Tribunal was clearly an independent proceeding which must be decided in accordance with provisions of Code. [22]

4. Appellant was granted liberty to apply under proviso to Section 434 of Companies Act (added in 2018), to transfer winding up proceeding pending before High Court of Delhi to NCLT, which could then be treated as a proceeding under Section 9 of Code. [23]

25

K. KISHAN VS. VIJAY NIRMAN COMPANY PVT. LTD. (14.08.2018 – SC)

Relevant Section: Arbitration and Conciliation Act, 1996 - Section 4, Section 9, Section 9(5), Section 34, Section 34(3), Section 37; Limitation Act, 1963 - Section 14; Insolvency and Bankruptcy Code, 2016 - Section 2, Section 3(11), Section 8, Section 8(1), Section 8(2), Section 9, Section 9(2), Section 9(5), Section 238; Insolvency and Bankruptcy (Application to Adjudicating Authority) Rules, 2016 - Rule 98(2)

Hon'ble Judges/Coram: Rohinton Fali Nariman and Indu Malhotra, JJ.

Number of PDF Pages in Original Judgement: 10

Citation: I(2019)BC3(SC), 2018(5)BomCR705, 2019(4) CHN (SC) 10, [2018]146CLA1(SC), (2018)4CompLJ168(SC), 2019(1) CTC484, (2018)8MLJ177, 2018(4)RCR(Civil)197, 2018(10) SCALE256, [2018]150SCL110(SC), MANU/SC/0872/2018

Case Note: Arbitration - Operational debt - Pending of award - Section 34 of Arbitration and Conciliation Act, 1996 - Disputes arose between parties in respect to contract entered between parties and same were referred to Arbitral Tribunal, which delivered its Award - Petition under Section 34 of Act was filed for setting aside of award - Thereafter petition was filed under Section 9 of Insolvency and

Bankruptcy Code, 2016 to Company Law Tribunal who held that fact that Section 34 petition was pending was irrelevant for reason that claim stood admitted, and there was no stay of Award - On appeal, Appellate Tribunal confirmed order passed by Tribunal - Hence, present appeal - Whether Insolvency and Bankruptcy Code, 2016 could be invoked in respect of operational debt where Arbitral Award had been passed against operational debtor, which had not yet been finally adjudicated upon.

Appeal Allowed

Facts: The disputes and differences arose between the parties in respect to contract entered between parties and the same were referred to an Arbitral Tribunal, which delivered its Award. Section 34 petition was filed under the Arbitration and Conciliation Act, 1996 challenging the said Award. Thereafter that a petition was filed under Section 9 of the Code to National Company Law Tribunal who held that fact that a Section 34 petition was pending was irrelevant for the reason that the claim stood admitted, and there was no stay of the Award. On appeal, the Appellate Tribunal held that since Form V of Part 5 of the Insolvency & Bankruptcy Rules, 2016 requires particulars of an order of an arbitral panel adjudicating on the default, this would have to be treated as a record of an operational debt, as a result of which the petition would have to be admitted, as was correctly done by the Tribunal.

Hon'ble Apex Court held, while allowing the appeal:

i. It was clear that operational creditors could not use the Insolvency Code either prematurely or for extraneous considerations or as a substitute for debt enforcement procedures. The alarming result of an operational debt contained in an arbitral award for a small amount of say, two lakhs of rupees, could not possibly jeopardize an otherwise solvent company worth several crores of rupees. Such a company would be well within its rights to state that it is challenging the Arbitral Award passed against it, and the mere factum of challenge would be sufficient to state that it disputes the Award. Such a case would clearly come within case of Mobilox Innovations, being a case of a pre-existing ongoing dispute between the parties. The Code could not be used in terrorem to extract this sum of money of two lakhs rupees even though it may not be finally payable as adjudication proceedings in respect thereto were still pending. The object of the Code, at least insofar as operational creditors are concerned, was to put the insolvency process against a corporate debtor only in clear cases where a real dispute between the parties as to the debt owed did not exist. [13]

ii. It may hasten to add that there may be cases where a Section 34 petition challenging an Arbitral Award may clearly and unequivocally be barred by limitation, in that it can be demonstrated to the Court that the period of ninety days plus the discretionary period of thirty days had clearly expired, after which either no petition Under Section 34 of Act had been filed or a belated petition under Section 34 of Act had been filed. It was only in such clear cases that the insolvency process may then be put into operation. [19]

iii. The Appellate Tribunal was in error in referring to Section 238 of the Code. Section 238 of the Code would apply in case there is an inconsistency between the Code and the Arbitration Act in the present case. On the contrary, the Award passed under the Arbitration Act together with the steps taken for its challenge would only make it clear that the operational debt, in the present case, happen to be a disputed one. [22]

26

BABULAL VARDHARJI GURJAR VS. VEER GURJAR ALUMINIUM INDUSTRIES PVT. LTD. AND ORS. (14.08.2020 – SC)

Relevant Section: Insolvency And Bankruptcy Code, 2016 - Section 7

Hon'ble Judges/Coram: Dinesh Maheshwari and A.M. Khanwilkar, JJ.

Number of PDF Pages in Original Judgement: 39

Citation: MANU/SC/0589/2020

Case Note: Company - Insolvency Resolution Process - Barred by time - Section 7 of Insolvency and Bankruptcy Code, 2016 - Respondent No. 2 while stating its capacity as financial creditor, for being assignee of loans and advances disbursed by creditor bank to corporate debtor, filed application under Section 7 of Code before Adjudicating Authority and sought initiation of Corporate Insolvency Resolution Process (CIRP) in respect of Respondent No. 1 - Adjudicating Authority admitted application and appointed interim resolution professional - Being aggrieved by said order, Appellant preferred appeal before Appellate Tribunal and contended against maintainability of application moved by Respondent No. 2 - Appeal so filed by Appellant was summarily dismissed by Appellate

Tribunal - However, order so passed by Appellate Tribunal was not approved by this Court after finding that issue relating to limitation, was not decided by Appellate Tribunal - Hence, matter was remanded to Appellate Tribunal for dealing with issue of limitation - Appellate Tribunal had held that neither application under Section 7 as made was barred by limitation nor claim of Respondent No. 2 was so barred - Hence, present appeal - Whether application made by Respondent No. 2 under Section 7 of Code seeking initiation of CIRP was clearly barred by limitation.

Appeal Partly Allowed

Facts:

The Respondent No. 2 while stating its capacity as the financial creditor, for being the assignee of the loans and advances disbursed by creditor bank to the corporate debtor, filed the said application under Section 7 of the Code before the Adjudicating Authority and sought initiation of CIRP in respect of the Respondent No. 1. After having considered the submissions on behalf of the financial creditor and the corporate debtor, the Adjudicating Authority, admitted the application so made by the financial creditor and appointed an interim resolution professional. Being aggrieved by the said order, the Appellant preferred an appeal before NCLAT and contended against maintainability of the application moved by the Respondent No. 2. The appeal so filed by the Appellant was summarily dismissed by the Appellate Tribunal by its order. However, the order so passed by the Appellate Tribunal was not approved by this Court in the judgment passed in Civil Appeal after finding that the issue relating to limitation, though raised, was not decided by the Appellate Tribunal. Hence, the matter was remanded to NCLAT for specifically dealing with the issue of limitation. After such remand, the Appellate Tribunal, by its impugned order, has held that neither the application under Section 7 as made in this case was barred by limitation nor the claim of the Respondent No. 2 was so barred and has, therefore, again dismissed the appeal.

Hon'ble Apex Court held, while allowing the appeal:

i. Even if it be assumed that the principles relating to acknowledgement as per Section 18 of the Limitation Act were applicable for extension of time for the purpose of the application under Section 7 of the Code, neither the said provision and principles come in operation in the present case nor they enure to the benefit of Respondent No. 2 for the fundamental reason that in the application made before NCLT, the Respondent No. 2 specifically stated the date of default being the date of NPA. It remains indisputable that neither any other date of default had been stated in the application nor any suggestion about any acknowledgement had been made. As noticed, even in Part-V of the application, the Respondent No. 2 was required to state the particulars of financial debt with documents and evidence on record. In the variety of descriptions which could have been given by the Applicant in the said Part-V of the application and even in residuary point therein, nothing was at all stated at any place about the so called acknowledgment or any other date of default. [33]

ii. Therefore, on the admitted fact situation of the present case, where only the date of default as had been stated for the purpose of maintaining the application under Section 7 of the Code, and not even a foundation was laid in the application for suggesting any acknowledgement or any other date of default, the submissions sought to be developed on behalf of the Respondent No. 2 at the later stage could not be permitted. Indisputably, in the present case, the Respondent No. 2 never came out with any pleading other than stating the date of default in the application. That being the position, no case for extension of period of limitation was available to be examined. In other words, even if Section 18 of the Limitation Act and principles thereof were applicable, the same would not apply to the application under consideration in the present case, looking to the very averment regarding default therein and for want of any other averment in regard to acknowledgement. [33.1]

iii. Though NCLAT had referred to the pendency of the application under Section 19 of the Act of 1993 as also the fact that corporate debtor had made a prayer for OTS but, had not recorded any specific finding about the effect of these factors. Only two reasons essentially appear to have weighed with NCLAT to hold that the application in question was within limitation. One, that the right to apply under Section 7 of the Code accrued to the Respondent financial creditor when the Code came into force; and second, that the period of limitation for recovery of possession of the mortgaged property is twelve years. The reasonings so adopted by NCLAT did not stand in conformity with the law declared by this Court and could only be disapproved. [35]

iv. The question as to whether date of enforcement of the Code provides the starting point of limitation for an application under Section 7 of the Code and hence, the application in question, was within limitation, was not even worth devoting much time. A bare look of the impugned order leaves nothing to guess that such observations by the Appellate Tribunal had only been assumptive in nature without any foundation and without any basis. There was nothing in the Code to even remotely indicate if the period of limitation for the purpose of an application under Section 7 was to commence from the date of commencement of the Code itself. Similarly, nothing provided in the Limitation Act could be taken as the basis to support the proposition so stated by the Appellate Tribunal. In fact, such observations had been in the teeth of law declared by this Court in the case of B.K. Educational Services. [36]

v. The application made by the Respondent No. 2 under Section 7 of the Code seeking initiation of CIRP in respect of the corporate debtor with specific assertion of the date of default was clearly barred by limitation for having been filed much later than the period of three years from the date of default as stated in the application. The NCLT having not examined the question of limitation, the NCLAT having decided the question of limitation on entirely irrelevant considerations and the attempt on the part of the Respondents to save the limitation with reference to the principles of acknowledgment having been found unsustainable, the impugned orders deserve to be set aside and the application filed by the Respondent No. 2 deserves to be rejected as being barred by limitation. [38]

Legal Latin Terms Group 11

lex loci - The law of the place where the cause of action arose

lis pendens - Litigation pending

locus delicti - The place of the crime

locus sigilli - The place for the seal

mala - Bad

mala fides - Bad faith

mala in se - An act that is morally wrong

mala praxis - Malpractice

mala prohibita - An act declared as criminal by statute

mala animo - Acting with evil intent

mandamus - A writ used to compel an official to perform a required act

27

JK Jute Mill Mazdoor Morcha vs. Juggilal Kamlapat Jute Mills Company Ltd. and Ors. (30.04.2019 – SC)

Relevant Section: Insolvency And Bankruptcy Code, 2016 - Section 3(23); Section 5(20); - Section 5(21); Trade Unions Act, 1926 - Section 2(h); Section 2(g); Trade Unions Act, 1926 - Section 8; Section 13; Section 15(c); Section 15(d)

Hon'ble Judges/Coram: Rohinton Fali Nariman and Vineet Saran, JJ.

Number of PDF Pages in Original Judgement: 8

Citation: AIR2019SC2138, 2019 4 AWC3160SC, III(2019)BC1(SC), 2019(3) CHN (SC) 169, [2019]150CLA279(SC), 2019(3)CTC715, 2019(2)RCR(Civil)997, 2019(7)SCALE136, (2019)11SCC332, 2019 (6) SCJ 411, [2019]154SCL1(SC), MANU/SC/0626/2019

Case Note: Insolvency - Operational creditor - Trade union - Representation - Sections 8 and 3(23) of Insolvency and Bankruptcy Code, 2016 (Code) and Sections 8 and 13 of the Trade Unions Act, 1926 and Rule 6, Form 5 of the Insolvency and Bankruptcy (Application to Adjudicating Authority) Rules, 2016 - Appeal was against impugned order of National Company Law Appellate Tribunal [NCLAT] stating that each worker may file an individual application before the NCLT and a trade union not being covered as an operational creditor - Whether a trade union could be said to be an operational creditor for purpose of Code, 2016.

Appeal Allowed

Facts: The facts of the present case reveal a long-drawn saga of a jute mill being closed and reopened several times until finally, it has been closed for good on 7th March, 2014. Proceedings were pending under Act, 1985. On 14th March, 2017, the Appellant issued a demand notice on behalf of roughly 3000 workers under Section 8 of the Code for outstanding dues of workers. This was replied to by Respondent No. 1. The National Company Law Tribunal [NCLT] held that, a trade union not being covered as an operational creditor, the petition would have to be dismissed. By the impugned order, the National Company Law Appellate Tribunal [NCLAT] did likewise and dismissed the appeal filed by the Appellant, stating that each worker may file an individual application before the NCLT. Appellant argued that, provisions of the Code would lead to the result that, a trade union would be an operational creditor within the meaning of the Code. Even otherwise, a purposive interpretation ought to be granted, as has been done in various recent judgments to the provisions of the Code, and that therefore, such an application by a registered trade union filed as an operational creditor would be maintainable.

Hon'ble Apex Court held, while allowing the appeal

A trade union is certainly an entity established under a statute-namely, the Trade Unions Act, and would therefore fall within the definition of "person" under Sections 3(23) of the Code. This being so, it is clear that an "operational debt", meaning a claim in respect of employment, could certainly be made by a person duly authorised to make such claim on behalf of a workman. Rule 6, Form 5 of the Insolvency and Bankruptcy (Application to Adjudicating Authority) Rules, 2016 also recognises the fact that claims may be made not only in an individual capacity, but also conjointly. Further, a registered trade union recognised by Section 8 of Act, makes it clear that it can sue and be sued as a body corporate under Section 13 of that Act. Equally, the general fund of the trade union, which inter alia is from collections from workmen who are its members, can certainly be spent on the conduct of disputes involving a member or members thereof or for the prosecution of a legal proceeding to which the trade union is a party, and which is undertaken for the purpose of protecting the rights arising out of the relation of its members with their employer, which would include wages and other sums due from the employer to workmen. [6]

A registered trade union which is formed for the purpose of regulating the relations between workmen and their employer can maintain a petition as an operational creditor on behalf of its members. [10]

The NCLAT, by the impugned judgment, is not correct in refusing to go into whether the trade union would come within the definition of "person" under Section 3(23) of the Code. Equally, the NCLAT is not correct in stating that a trade union would not be an operational creditor as no services are rendered by the trade union to the corporate debtor. The trade union represents its members who are workers, to whom dues may be owed by the employer, which are certainly debts owed for services rendered by each individual workman, who are collectively represented by the trade union. Equally, to state that for each workman there will be a separate cause of action, a separate claim, and a separate date of default would ignore the fact that, a joint petition could be filed under Rule 6 read with Form 5 of the Rules, 2016, with authority from several workmen to one of them to file such petition on behalf of all. The appeal is allowed and the judgment of the NCLAT is set aside. The matter is now remanded to the NCLAT who will decide the appeal on merits expeditiously as this matter has been pending for quite some time. [11]

Ratio Decidendi: A registered trade union can maintain a petition as an operational creditor on behalf of its members

28

VINAY KUMAR MITTAL AND ORS. VS. DEWAN HOUSING FINANCE CORPORATION LTD. AND ORS. (31.01.2020 – SC)

Relevant Section: Insolvency And Bankruptcy (insolvency And Liquidation Proceedings Of Financial Service Providers And Application To Adjudicating Authority) Rules, 2019 - Rule 5, Rule 6; Insolvency and Bankruptcy Board of India (Insolvency Resolution Process for Corporate Persons) Regulations, 2016 - Regulation 6; Insolvency And Bankruptcy Code, 2016 - Section 14, Section 15, Section 21(6A), Section 227, Section 239(2); National Housing Bank Act, 1987 - Section 36, Section 36(A)

Hon'ble Judges/Coram: L. Nageswara Rao and Deepak Gupta, JJ.

Number of PDF Pages in Original Judgement: 5

Citation: I(2020)BC552(SC), 2020(2)BomCR412, [2020]160SCL120(SC), MANU/SC/0118/2020

Case Note: Company - Interim order - Challenge thereto - Appeals were filed against interim orders passed by High Court which restrained Respondent No. 1 from making further payments disbursements to any unsecured creditors and secured creditors -

Whether repayments of deposits of Appellants should be given preference over contractual claims of debenture holders

Disposed off

Facts: Reliance Nippon Life Asset Management Ltd. ('Respondent No. 4') filed Commercial Suit for recovery of a sum of Rs. 479,31,29,113 along with interest at the rate of 18 per cent. The case of Respondent No. 4 is that it subscribed to Non-Convertible Debentures (NCDs) of Dewan Housing Finance Corporation Limited (DHFL, 'Respondent No. 1') to the tune of Rs. 63,41,72,000/-, that were issued through a public offer. In 2017-2018, Respondent No. 4 further subscribed to NCDs of Respondent No. 1, aggregating to Rs. 365 crores, issued on a private placement basis. Respondent No. 4 became entitled to early redemption of private placement NCDs in March, 2019 due to the down grading in ratings of the NCDs issued by Respondent No. 1. Respondent No. 1 failed to pay the entire amount towards the early redemption. By an order, the High Court restrained Respondent No. 1 from making further payments disbursements to any unsecured creditors and secured creditors except in cases where payments are to be made on a pro-rata basis to all secured creditors out of its current and future receivables in preference to the payments owed to Respondent No. 4. By an order dated 10.10.2019, the High Court directed the continuance of the order passed on 30.09.2019 till the disposal of the motion. Similar orders were passed in the interim applications filed in the other commercial suits by orders dated 17.10.2019, 08.11.2019 and 13th November, 2019. It was clarified by the High Court on 13th November, 2019 that Respondent No. 1 shall not be prevented from making any payments overdue or payable under the assignment agreements in favour of any or all such banks or assignees of loans. The Appellants are depositors who invested in fixed deposits with the Respondent No. 1-DHFL. Having been aggrieved by the interim orders passed by the High Court and the Debts Recovery Tribunal-I, Mumbai restraining Respondent No. 1 from making any payments towards their fixed deposits, the Appellants challenged the orders of the High Court with the leave of this Court.

Hon'ble Apex Court held, while disposing of the appeal

1. Learned Senior Counsel appearing for the Appellants expressed his apprehension that the interim orders dated 10.10.2019 as modified by the order dated 13th November, 2019 might come in the way of consideration of the claims that are made by the depositors before the Committee of Creditors and the Administrator. After hearing the learned Counsel for the Administrator and the RBI on this point, present Court is of the opinion that the claims that are made by the depositors shall be considered by the Committee of Creditors and the Administrator without being influenced by the orders passed by the High Court on 10.10.2019 as modified by order dated 13th November, 2019, as well as the order passed by the Debts Recovery Tribunal. [13]

2. It is further submitted that the decision taken by the Committee of Creditors on 30.12.2019 by which the Administrator was permitted to carry on the lending operations of the first Respondent without paying the depositors is arbitrary and illegal. [14]

3. It is not necessary to examine the merit of the contentions made by the learned Senior Counsel. The depositors are being represented by the Authorized Representative before the Committee of Creditors. It is open to the Appellants to raise all points and contentions before the Committee of Creditors, the Administrator and if necessary, the NCLT. There are nearly one lakh depositors who have invested their life time earnings with Respondent No. 1. Some of the deposits have matured and some of the depositors are critically ill. The concerns of the depositors and their rights shall be considered in accordance with law. [15]

29

SWARAJ INFRASTRUCTURE PVT. LTD. VS. KOTAK MAHINDRA BANK LTD. (29.01.2019 – SC)

Relevant Section: Recovery of Debts Due to Banks and Financial Institutions Act, 1993 - Section 17; - Section 18; Companies Act, 1956 - Section 434(1)(b), Insolvency and Bankruptcy Code, 2016; Constitution of India - Article 226, Constitution of India - Article 227

Hon'ble Judges/Coram: Rohinton Fali Nariman and Navin Sinha, JJ.

Number of PDF Pages in Original Judgement: 16

Citation: 2020(1)ALLMR938, 2019 (135) ALR 730, II(2019) BC47(SC), 2019(2)BomCR873, 2019(2) CHN (SC) 1, [2019]148CLA564(SC), [2019]213CompCas99(SC), 2019(3) CTC782, 123(1)CWN220, 2019(2)RCR(Civil)66, 2019(2) SCALE171, (2019)3SCC620, [2019]152SCL242(SC), (2019)3WBLR(SC)444, MANU/SC/0095/2019

Case Note: Company - Recovery of amount - Right of a secured creditor - Winding up petition - Section 434 of Companies Act, 1956 - Present case involved right of a secured creditor to file a winding up petition after such secured creditor had obtained a decree from Debts Recovery Tribunal [DRT] and a recovery certificate based thereon - Whether a secured creditor could maintain a winding up petition in fact of present case.

Appeal Dismissed

Facts: Respondent, Kotak Mahindra Bank Limited, advanced various loans to companies in question. Outstanding amount against these companies as on date, together with interest, was stated to be in region of 48 crores. Respondent approached Debts Recovery Tribunal, Mumbai by filing three separate original applications to recover debt owed to them. Debts Recovery Tribunal delivered three separate judgments allowing applications filed by Respondent bank. Apparently, said orders were final as no appeals had been preferred to Debts Recovery Appellate Tribunal [DRAT]. Recovery certificates for said amounts were then issued by Recovery Officer under Section 19(19) of the Recovery of Debts Due to Banks and Financial Institutions Act, 1993 [Recovery of Debts Act]. Various attempts were made to auction properties that were security for loans granted, but each of these attempts had yielded no results. In meanwhile, Respondent issued statutory notices dated 15th April, 2015 under Sections 433 and 434 of Companies Act, 1956. As no payments were forthcoming, a company petition was filed before Bombay High Court. By an order, said petition was admitted as companies in question were said to be commercially insolvent. In appeals that were filed to Division Bench of High Court, main point argued was that once a secured creditor had obtained an order from DRT, and a recovery certificate had been issued thereupon, such secured creditor could not file a winding up petition as Recovery of Debts Act was a special Act which vested exclusive jurisdiction in DRT. Also, a secured creditor could file a winding up petition only on giving up its security, which had not been done in present case. These contentions did not find favour with Division Bench who then dismissed appeals in question.

Hon'ble Apex Court held, while dismissing the appeal

1. When it came to a winding up proceeding under Companies Act, 1956, since such a proceeding is not "for recovery of debts"

due to banks, bar contained in Section 18 read with Section 34 of Recovery of Debts Act would not apply to winding up proceedings under Companies Act, 1956. [13]

2. Section 434(1)(b) was attracted only if execution or other process was issued in respect of an order of a Tribunal in favour of a creditor of company was returned unsatisfied in whole or in part. This was only one of three instances in which a company shall be deemed to be unable to pay its debts. If fact situation fitted Sub-clause (b) of Section 434(1), then a company might be said to be deemed to be unable to pay its debts. However, this did not mean that, each one of sub-clauses of Section 434(1) were mutually exclusive in sense that, once Section 434(1)(b) applied, Section 434(1)(a) ceased to be applicable. Also, on facts of this case, company petition was filed only on 3rd July, 2015, pursuant to a notice under Section 433 of Companies Act, 1956 dated 15th April, 2015. This petition was filed under Section 433(e) read with Section 434(1)(a) of Companies Act, 1956. At the stage ,at which petition was filed, it could not possibly have been filed under Section 434(1)(b) of Companies Act, 1956, as execution or other process in form of a recovery certificate had not been issued by Recovery Officer till 12th August, 2015, i.e., till after company petition was filed. [19]

3. It was not open for persons like Appellant to resist a winding up petition which was otherwise maintainable without there being any bona fide defence to same. When secured creditors like Respondent were driven from pillar to post to recover what was legitimately due to them, in attempting to avail of more than one remedy at same time, they did not "blow hot and cold", but they blow hot and hotter. Appeals dismissed. [20]

30

STATE BANK OF INDIA VS. JAH DEVELOPERS PVT. LTD. AND ORS. (08.05.2019 – SC)

Relevant Section: Advocate Act, 1961 - Section 30, Arbitration Act, 1940, Constitution Of India - Article 19(1), Article 21, Article 22(3), Article 136, Article 136(1), Industrial Disputes Act, 1947 - Section 10A, Section 21, Section 22, Insolvency And Bankruptcy Code, 2016 - Section 29A, Punjab Welfare Officers Recruitment and Conditions of Service Rules, 1952 - Rule 6(6), Railway Protection Force Rules, 1987 - Rule 153.8

Hon'ble Judges/Coram: Rohinton Fali Nariman and Vineet Saran, JJ.

Number of PDF Pages in Original Judgement: 14

Citation: AIR2019SC2854, 2019(5)ALD107, 2020 (140) ALR 240, III(2019)BC290(SC), 2019(4)BomCR15, 2019(4) CHN (SC) 73, 2020- 3-LW215, 2019(6)MhLj406, 2019(4)MPLJ290, 2019(3) RCR(Civil)114, 2019(7)SCALE725, (2019)6SCC787, 2019 (7) SCJ 426, [2019]154SCL72(SC), (2019)4WBLR(SC)391, MANU/SC/0769/2019

Case Note: Banking - Wilful defaulter - Right to represent - Section 30 of Advocates' Act, 1961 (Advocates Act) and Section 29A of the Insolvency and Bankruptcy Code, 2016 and Article 19(1)

(g) of Constitution of India, 1950 - Appeal was against impugned order of Delhi High Court holding that, two in-house committees could be considered to be tribunals, and that therefore, a lawyer had right to represent his client before such in-house committees - Whether, when a person was declared to be a wilful defaulter under Circulars of Reserve Bank of India (RBI), such person was entitled to be represented by a lawyer of its choice before such declaration is made - Whether an oral hearing was required under Revised Circular dated 1st July, 2015.

Appeal Allowed

Facts: The RBI Circular dated 1st July, 2013 is described as a Master Circular on Wilful Defaulters [Master Circular] and is addressed to all scheduled commercial banks (excluding Regional Rural Banks (RRBs) and Local Area Banks (LABs)), and to All India Notified Financial Institutions. RBI issued another Master Circular consolidating instructions on how all scheduled commercial banks and notified financial institutions are to deal with wilful defaulters [Revised Circular]. The definition of wilful default is substantially the same as in the earlier Master Circular. As nobody appeared on behalf of the Respondents in the Civil Appeal Shri Parag Tripathi, learned Senior Advocate appointed to assist as Amicus Curiae. Shri Tripathi has argued that Section 30 of Advocates Act makes it clear that, an advocate has the right to practice before any tribunal or person legally authorised to take evidence. Appellants cited a number of judgments to show that, the right to legal representation is no part of the right of natural justice. They also assailed the judgment of the Delhi High Court, stating that, by no stretch of imagination could the in-house committees referred to in the RBI Circulars be said to be tribunals as there is no investment of any judicial power by the State in these in-house committees.

Hon'ble Apex Court held, while allowing the appeal

1. State's judicial power is the power to decide a lis between the parties after gathering evidence and applying the law, as a result

of which, a binding decision is then reached. This is far from the present case as the in-house committees are not vested with any judicial power at all, their powers being administrative powers given to in-house committees to gather facts and then arrive at a result. Secondly, it cannot be said that the Circulars in any manner vests the State's judicial power in such in-house committees. On this ground, therefore, the view of Delhi High Court is not correct, and no lawyer has any right under Section 30 of the Advocates Act to appear before the in-house committees so mentioned. Further, the said committees are also not persons legally authorised to take evidence by statute or subordinate legislation, and on this score also, no lawyer would have any right under Section 30 of the Advocates Act to appear before the same. [12]

2. Revised Circular dated 1st July, 2015 makes a departure from the earlier Master Circular in that an oral hearing may only be given by the First Committee at the first stage if it is so found necessary. Given the scheme of the Revised Circular, it is difficult to state that oral hearing is mandatory. It is even more difficult to state that in all cases oral hearings must be given, or else the principles of natural justice are breached. A number of judgments have held that natural justice is a flexible tool that is used in order that a person or authority arrive at a just result. Such result can be arrived at in many cases without oral hearing but on written representations given by parties, after considering which, a decision is then arrived at. [13]

3. There is no right to be represented by a lawyer in the in-house proceedings contained in paragraph 3 of the Revised Circular dated 1st July, 2015, as it is clear that, the events of wilful default as mentioned in paragraph 2.1.3 would only relate to the individual facts of each case. Whether a default is intentional, deliberate, and calculated is again a question of fact which the lender may put to the borrower in a show cause notice to elicit the borrower's submissions on the same. However, Article 19(1)(g) is attracted in the facts of the present case as the moment

a person is declared to be a wilful defaulter, the impact on its fundamental right to carry on business is direct and immediate. This is for the reason that, no additional facilities can be granted by any bank/financial institutions, and entrepreneurs/promoters would be barred from institutional finance for five years. Banks/financial institutions can even change the management of the wilful defaulter, and a promoter/director of a wilful defaulter cannot be made promoter or director of any other borrower company. Equally, under Section 29A of Code, 2016, a wilful defaulter cannot even apply to be a resolution applicant. Given these drastic consequences, it is clear that the Revised Circular, being in public interest, must be construed reasonably. This being so, and given the fact that paragraph 3 of the Master Circular dated 1st July, 2013 permitted the borrower to make a representation within 15 days of the preliminary decision of the First Committee, present Court is of view that, Committee comprising of the Executive Director and two other senior officials, being the First Committee, after following paragraph 3(b) of the Revised Circular dated 1st July, 2015, must give its order to the borrower as soon as it is made. The borrower can then represent against such order within a period of 15 days to the Review Committee. Such written representation can be a full representation on facts and law (if any). The Review Committee must then pass a reasoned order on such representation which must then be served on the borrower. Given the fact that, the earlier Master Circular dated 1st July, 2013 itself considered such steps to be reasonable, all these steps are incorporated into the Revised Circular dated 1st July, 2015. The impugned judgment is, therefore, set aside. Appeals allowed. [21]

Ratio Decidendi: A borrower does not have a right to be represented by a lawyer before he is declared a wilful defaulter by In-House committee.

31

SWISS RIBBONS PVT. LTD. AND ORS. VS. UNION OF INDIA (UOI) AND ORS. (25.01.2019 – SC)

Relevant Section: Sections 12A, 29A, 240A, 60, 53, 30 and 31 of Insolvency and Bankruptcy Code, 2016 [Code], Article 14 of Constitution of India and Section 433(e) of Companies Act, 1956

Hon'ble Judges/Coram: Rohinton Fali Nariman and Navin Sinha, JJ.

Number of PDF Pages in Original Judgement: 14

Citation: AIR2019SC 739, 2019(2)ALD147, I(2019)BC 259(SC), [2019]148C LA419(SC), [2019]213C ompC as198(SC), (2019)1C ompLJ273-364(SC), 2019(2)C TC 168, 123(1)C WN87, 2019(2)SC ALE5, (2019)4SC C 17, 2019 (7) SC J 579, [2019]152SC L365(SC), MANU/SC/0079/2019

Case Note: Insolvency - Validity of provisions - Sections 12A, 29A, 240A, 60, 53, 30 and 31 of Insolvency and Bankruptcy Code, 2016 [Code], Article 14 of Constitution of India and Section 433(e) of Companies Act, 1956 - Present petitions assailed constitutional validity of various provisions of Code - Whether members of National Company Law Tribunal [NCLT] and certain members of National Company Law Appellate Tribunal [NCLAT], apart from President, had been appointed contrary to present Court's judgment in Madras Bar Association (III) - Whether classification between financial creditor and operational creditor was discriminatory or violative of Article 14 of Constitution of India - Whether Section 12A was not violative of Article 14 of Constitution - Whether vested rights of erstwhile promoters to participate in recovery process of a corporate debtor had been impaired by retrospective application of Section 29A of Code - Whether Section 53 of Code violated Article 14 of Constitution.

Disposed off

Facts: Constitutional validity of various provisions of Code was subject matter in present appeal. First and foremost argument in present case was that, members of National Company Law Tribunal [NCLT] and certain members of National Company Law Appellate Tribunal [NCLAT], apart from President, had been appointed contrary to this Court's judgment in Madras Bar Association v. Union of India, [Madras Bar Association (III)], and that therefore, this being so, all orders that were passed by such members, being passed contrary to judgment of this Court in aforesaid case, ought to be set aside. Further, such members ought to be restrained from passing any orders in future. Administrative support for all tribunals should be from Ministry of Law and Justice. Since the NCLAT, as an appellate court, had a seat only at New Delhi, this would render remedy inefficacious as persons would have to travel from Tamil Nadu, Calcutta, and Bombay to New Delhi, whereas earlier, they could have approached respective High Courts in their States. This again is directly contrary to Madras Bar Association v. Union of India, [Madras Bar Association (II)]. Apart from aforesaid technical objection, it had assailed legislative scheme that was contained in Section 7 of Code, stating that there was no real difference between financial creditors and operational creditors. According to him, both types of creditors would give either money in terms of loans or money's worth in terms of goods and services. Thus, there was no intelligible differentia between the two types of creditors, regard being had to object sought to be achieved by Code, namely, insolvency resolution, and if that is not possible, then ultimately, liquidation. It was argued that, assuming that a valid distinction existed between financial and operational creditors, there was hostile discrimination against operational creditors. First and foremost, unless they amount to 10% of aggregate of amount of debt owed, they had no voice in committee of creditors. In any case, Sections 21 and 24 of Code were discriminatory and manifestly arbitrary in that operational creditors did not have even a single vote in committee of creditors which had very important functions to perform in resolution process of corporate debtors. Further, establishment of information utilities that were set up under Code were also assailed. Next argument was that Section 12A of Code was contrary to the directions of this Court in its order in Uttara Foods and Feeds Pvt. Ltd. v. Mona Pharmachem. Lastly, a four-fold attack was raised against Section 29A, in particular, Clause (c) thereof. First and foremost, Shri Rohatgi stated that the vested rights of erstwhile promoters to participate in the recovery process of a corporate debtor have been impaired by retrospective application of Section 29A. Another argument that was made was that under Section 29A(c), a person's account might be classified as a non-performing asset [NPA] in accordance with guidelines of Reserve Bank of India [RBI], despite him not being a wilful defaulter. Also, period of one year referred to in Clause (c) was again wholly arbitrary and without any basis either in rationality or in law.

Hon'ble Apex Court held, while disposing of the appeal

1. On 3rd January, 2018, Companies Amendment Act, 2017 was brought into force by which Section 412 of Companies Act, 2013 was amended regarding Selection of Members of Tribunal and Appellate Tribunal. Members of the Tribunal and Technical Members of Appellate Tribunal shall be appointed on recommendation of a Selection Committee consisting of-- (a) Chief Justice of India or his nominee-- Chairperson; (b) a senior Judge of the Supreme Court or Chief Justice of High Court--Member;(c) Secretary in the Ministry of Corporate Affairs-- Member; and (d) Secretary in the Ministry of Law and Justice-- Member. Where in a meeting of Selection Committee, there was equality of votes on any matter, Chairperson shall have a casting

vote. This was brought into force by a Notification dated 9th February,2018. However, an additional affidavit had been filed during course of these proceedings by Union of India. This affidavit made it clear that, acting in compliance with directions of Supreme Court in judgments of Madras Bar Association (I) and Madras Bar Association (III), a Selection Committee was constituted to make appointments of Members of the NCLT in year 2015 itself. [14]

2. Regarding submission that, NCLAT Bench only at Delhi, learned Attorney General had assured that, judgment in case of Madras Bar Association (II) would be followed and Circuit Benches would be established as soon as it was practicable. Union of India was directed to set up Circuit Benches of NCLAT within a period of 6 months from today. [16]

3. Regarding argument that, Tribunals were functioning under wrong ministry, even though eight years have passed since date of judgment in Madras Bar Association (I), administrative support for these tribunals continued to be from Ministry of Corporate Affairs. This was required to be rectified at earliest. [17]

4. With regard to classification between financial creditor and operational creditor, since equality was only among equals, no discrimination resulted if Court could be shown that, there was an intelligible differentia which separated two kinds of creditors so long as there was some rational relation between creditors so differentiated, with object sought to be achieved by legislation. [20]

5. Argument of learned Counsel on behalf of Petitioners was that in point of fact, there was no intelligible differentia having relation to objects sought to be achieved by Code between financial and operational creditors and indeed, nowhere in world had this distinction been made. [25]

6. Most financial creditors, particularly banks and financial institutions, were secured creditors whereas most operational creditors were unsecured, payments for goods and services as

well as payments to workers not being secured by mortgaged documents and like. Distinction between secured and unsecured creditors was a distinction which had obtained since earliest of Companies Acts both in United Kingdom and in India. Nature of loan agreements with financial creditors was different from contracts with operational creditors for supplying goods and services. Financial creditors generally lend finance on a term loan or for working capital that enabled corporate debtor to either set up and/or operate its business. On other hand, contracts with operational creditors were relatable to supply of goods and services in operation of business. Financial contracts generally involve large sums of money. By way of contrast, operational contracts had dues whose quantum was generally less. In running of a business, operational creditors can be many as opposed to financial creditors, who lend finance for the set up or working of business. Also, financial creditors had specified repayment schedules, and defaults entitled financial creditors to recall a loan in totality. Contracts with operational creditors did not have any such stipulations. Also, forum in which dispute resolution took place was completely different. [27]

7. Most importantly, financial creditors were, from very beginning, involved with assessing viability of corporate debtor. They could, and therefore did, engage in restructuring of loan as well as reorganization of corporate debtor's business when there was financial stress, which were things operational creditors did not and could not do. Thus, preserving corporate debtor as a going concern, while ensuring maximum recovery for all creditors being objective of Code, financial creditors were clearly different from operational creditors and therefore, there was an intelligible differentia between two which had a direct relation to objects sought to be achieved by Code. [28]

8. Trigger for a financial creditor's application was non-payment of dues when they arose under loan agreements. It was for this reason that, Section 433(e) of Companies Act, 1956 had been repealed by Code and a change in approach had been brought

about. Legislative policy now was to move away from concept of "inability to pay debts" to "determination of default". Said shift enabled financial creditor to prove, based upon solid documentary evidence, that there was an obligation to pay debt and that debtor had failed in such obligation. [37]

9. Since, financial creditors were in business of money lending, banks and financial institutions were best equipped to assess viability and feasibility of business of corporate debtor. Even at time of granting loans, these banks and financial institutions undertake a detailed market study which included a techno-economic valuation report, evaluation of business, financial projection, etc. Since this detailed study had already been undertaken before sanctioning a loan, and since financial creditors had trained employees to assess viability and feasibility, they were in a good position to evaluate contents of a resolution plan. On other hand, operational creditors, who provide goods and services, were involved only in recovering amounts that were paid for such goods and services, and were typically unable to assess viability and feasibility of business. [44]

10. NCLAT had, while looking into viability and feasibility of resolution plans that were approved by committee of creditors, always gone into whether operational creditors were given roughly same treatment as financial creditors, and if they were not, such plans were either rejected or modified so that, operational creditors' rights were safeguarded. A resolution plan could not pass muster under Section 30(2)(b) read with Section 31, unless a minimum payment was made to operational creditors, being not less than liquidation value. [46]

11. Operational creditors were not discriminated against or that Article 14 had not been infracted either on ground of equals being treated unequally or on ground of manifest arbitrariness. [48]

12. Main thrust against provision of Section 12A was fact that, ninety per cent of committee of creditors had to allow withdrawal.

This high threshold had been explained in Insolvency Law Committee (ILC) Report as all financial creditors had to put their heads together to allow such withdrawal as, ordinarily, an omnibus settlement involving all creditors ought to be entered into. This explained why ninety per cent, which was substantially all financial creditors, had to grant their approval to an individual withdrawal or settlement. In any case, figure of ninety per cent, in absence of anything further to show that it was arbitrary, must pertain to domain of legislative policy, which had been explained by Report. If committee of creditors arbitrarily rejected a just settlement and/or withdrawal claim, NCLT, and thereafter, NCLAT could always set aside such decision under Section 60 of Code. Section 12A of Code also passed constitutional muster. [53]

13. It was settled law that, a statute was not retrospective merely because it affected existing rights; nor was it retrospective merely because a part of requisites for its action was drawn from a time antecedent to its passing. In ArcelorMittal, present Court had observed that, a resolution applicant had no vested right for consideration or approval of its resolution plan. [64]

14. No vested right was taken away by application of Section 29A. A resolution applicant who applied under Section 29A(c) had no vested right to apply for being considered as a resolution applicant. [65]

15. According to Petitioners, when immovable and movable property was sold in liquidation, it ought to be sold to any person, including persons who were not eligible to be resolution applicants as, often, it was erstwhile promoter who alone might purchase such properties piecemeal by public auction or by private contract. There was no vested right in an erstwhile promoter of a corporate debtor to bid for immovable and movable property of corporate debtor in liquidation. Further, given categories of persons who were ineligible under Section 29A, which included persons who were malfeasant, or persons who had fallen foul of law in some way, and persons who were unable to pay their debts

in grace period allowed, were further, by this proviso, interdicted from purchasing assets of corporate debtor whose debts they had either wilfully not paid or had been unable to pay. Legislative purpose which permeated Section 29A continued to permeate Section when it applied not merely to resolution applicants, but to liquidation also. [69]

16. Section 29A goes to eligibility to submit a resolution plan. A wilful defaulter, in accordance with guidelines of RBI, would be a person who though able to pay, did not pay. An NPA, on other hand, referred to account belonging to a person that was declared as such under guidelines issued by RBI. Legislative policy, therefore, was that a person who was unable to service its own debt beyond grace period referred to above, was unfit to be eligible to become a resolution applicant. This policy could not be found fault with. Neither could period of one year be found fault with, as this was a policy matter decided by the RBI and which emerges from its Master Circular, as during relevant period, an NPA was classified as a substandard asset. Ineligibility attached only after this one year period was over as NPA now got classified as a doubtful asset. [70]

17. Persons who act jointly or in concert with others were connected with business activity of resolution applicant. Similarly, all categories of persons mentioned in Section 5(24A) show that such persons must be "connected" with resolution applicant within meaning of Section 29A(j). This being case, said categories of persons who were collectively mentioned under caption "relative" obviously need to have a connection with business activity of resolution applicant. In absence of showing that, such person was "connected" with business of activity of resolution applicant, such person could not possibly be disqualified under Section 29A(j). All categories in Section 29A(j) dealt with persons, natural as well as artificial, who were connected with business activity of resolution applicant. Expression "related party", therefore, and "relative" contained in definition Sections must be read noscitur a sociis with categories of persons

mentioned in Explanation I, and so read, would include only persons who were connected with business activity of resolution applicant. [75]

18. An argument was also made that, expression "connected person" in Explanation I, Clause (ii) to Section 29A(j) could not possibly refer to a person who might be in management or control of business of corporate debtor in future. This would be arbitrary as explanation would then apply to an indeterminate person. This contention also required to be repelled as Explanation I sought to made it clear that, if a person was otherwise covered as a "connected person", this provision would also cover a person who was in management or control of business of the corporate debtor during implementation of a resolution plan. Therefore, any such person was not indeterminate at all, but was a person who was in saddle of business of corporate debtor either at an anterior point of time or even during implementation of resolution plan. [76]

19. Regarding exemption of micro, small, and medium enterprises from Section 29A of Code, ILC Report of March 2018 found that micro, small, and medium enterprises formed foundation of economy and were key drivers of employment, production, economic growth, entrepreneurship, and financial inclusion. [77]

20. Section 7 of Micro, Small and Medium Enterprises Development Act, 2006 classified enterprises depending upon whether they manufacture or produce goods, or were engaged in providing and rendering services as micro, small, or medium, depending upon certain investments made. [78]

21. Rationale for excluding such industries from eligibility criteria laid down in Section 29A(c) and 29A(h) was because qua such industries, other resolution applicants might not be forthcoming, which then would inevitably lead not to resolution, but to liquidation. Following upon Insolvency Law

Committee's Report, Section 240A had been inserted in Code with retrospective effect from 6th June, 2018. [80]

22. When Code had worked hardship to a class of enterprises, Committee constituted by Government, in overseeing working of Code, had been alive to such problems, and Government in turn had followed recommendations of Committee in enacting Section 240A. This was an important instance of how executive continued to monitor application of Code, and exempted a class of enterprises from application of some of its provisions in deserving cases. [81]

23. Repayment of financial debts infused capital into economy as banks and financial institutions were able, with money that had been paid back, to further lend such money to other entrepreneurs for their businesses. This rationale created an intelligible differentia between financial debts and operational debts, which were unsecured, which was directly related to object sought to be achieved by Code. In any case, workmen's dues, which were also unsecured debts, had traditionally been placed above most other debts. Thus, unsecured debts were of various kinds, and so long as there was some legitimate interest sought to be protected, having relation to object sought to be achieved by statute in question, Article 14 did not get infracted. Challenge to Section 53 of Code must also fail. [84]

Ratio Decidendi: A resolution applicant had no vested right for consideration or approval of its resolution plan

32

PIONEER URBAN LAND AND INFRASTRUCTURE LIMITED AND ORS. VS. UNION OF INDIA (UOI) AND ORS. (09.08.2019 – SC)

Relevant Section: Constitution Of India - Article 14; Article 19(1)(g); Article 300-A; Article 19(6) & Sections 5 and 7 of Insolvency and Bankruptcy Code, 2016

Hon'ble Judges/Coram: Rohinton Fali Nariman, Sanjiv Khanna and Surya Kant, JJ.

Number of PDF Pages in Original Judgement: 88

Citation: 2019(6)ABR257, AIR2019SC4055, IV(2019)BC183(SC), [2019]151CLA419(SC), [2019]217CompCas1(SC), (2019)4CompLJ202(SC), 2019(10)SCALE523, (2019)8SCC416, 2019 (8) SCJ 396, [2019]155SCL622(SC), MANU/SC/1071/2019

Case Note: Insolvency - Validity of amendment - Articles 300-A, 19 of Constitution of India, 1950 and Sections 5 and 7 of Insolvency and Bankruptcy Code, 2016 (Code)- Writ petitions had been filed challenging constitutional validity of amendments made to Code pursuant to a report prepared by the Insolvency Law Committee and amendments so made deem allottees of real estate projects to be "financial creditors" so that they may trigger the Code, under Section

7 thereof, against the real estate developer - Whether Amendment Act to the Code infringed Articles 14, 19(1)(g) read with Article 19(6), or 300-A of Constitution.

Appeals disposed off.

Facts: Writ petitions have been filed in present Court to challenge the constitutional validity of amendments made to the Code, pursuant to a report prepared by the Insolvency Law Committee dated 26th March, 2018 ("Insolvency Committee Report"). The amendments so made deem allottees of real estate projects to be "financial creditors" so that they may trigger the Code, under Section 7 thereof, against the real estate developer. In addition, being financial creditors, they are entitled to be represented in the Committee of Creditors by authorised representatives. The Code was passed by the Parliament on 28th May, 2016. Several petitions were then filed against real estate developers under the Code by allottees who had entered into "assured returns/committed returns" agreements with these developers, whereby, upon payment of a substantial portion of the total sale consideration upfront at the time of execution of the agreement, the developer undertook to pay a certain amount to allottees on a monthly basis from the date of execution of the agreement till the date of handing over of possession to the allottees. The National Company Law Appellate Tribunal ("NCLAT") on 21st July, 2017 in Nikhil Mehta and Sons (HUF) v. AMR Infrastructure Ltd., held that amounts raised by developers under assured return schemes had the "commercial effect of a borrowing", which became clear from the developer's annual returns in which the amount raised was shown as "commitment charges" under the head "financial costs". As a result, such allottees were held to be "financial creditors" within the meaning of Section 5(7) of the Code.

Hon'ble Apex Court held, while disposing of the appeal

1. As a matter of fact, the Code and Real Estate (Regulation and Development) Act, 2016 (RERA) operate in completely different spheres. The Code deals with a proceeding in rem in which the

focus is the rehabilitation of the corporate debtor. This is to take place by replacing the management of the corporate debtor by means of a resolution plan which must be accepted by 66% of the Committee of Creditors, which is now put at the helm of affairs, in deciding the fate of the corporate debtor. Such resolution plan then puts the same or another management in the saddle, subject to the provisions of the Code, so that the corporate debtor may be pulled out of the woods and may continue as a going concern, thus benefiting all stakeholders involved. It is only as a last resort that, winding up of the corporate debtor is resorted to, so that its assets may be liquidated and paid out in the manner provided by Section 53 of the Code. On the other hand, RERA protects the interests of the individual investor in real estate projects by requiring the promoter to strictly adhere to its provisions. The object of RERA is to see that real estate projects come to fruition within the stated period and to see that allottees of such projects are not left in the lurch and are finally able to realise their dream of a home, or be paid compensation if such dream is shattered, or at least get back monies that they had advanced towards the project with interest. At the same time, recalcitrant allottees are not to be tolerated, as they must also perform their part of the bargain, namely, to pay instalments as and when they become due and payable. Given the different spheres within which these two enactments operate, different parallel remedies are given to allottees-under RERA to see that, their flat/apartment is constructed and delivered to them in time, barring which compensation for the same and/or refund of amounts paid together with interest at the very least comes their way. If, however, the allottee wants that the corporate debtor's management itself be removed and replaced, so that the corporate debtor can be rehabilitated, he may prefer a Section 7 application under the Code. Another parallel remedy is available is recognised by RERA itself in the proviso to Section 71(1), by which an allottee may continue with an application already filed before the Consumer Protection fora, he being given the choice to withdraw such complaint and file an application before the adjudicating officer under RERA read with Section 88. [29]

2. It is impossible to say that, classifying real estate developers is not founded upon an intelligible differentia which distinguishes them from other operational creditors, nor is it possible to say that such classification is palpably arbitrary having no rational relation to the objects of the Code. It was vehemently argued by learned Counsel on behalf of the Petitioners that, if at all real estate developers were to be brought within the clutches of the Code, being like operational debtors, at best they could have been brought in under this rubric and not as financial debtors. Here again, what is unique to real estate developers vis-a-vis operational debts, is the fact that, in operational debts generally, when a person supplies goods and services, such person is the creditor and the person who has to pay for such goods and services is the debtor. In the case of real estate developers, the developer who is the supplier of the flat/apartment is the debtor as the home buyer/allottee funds his own apartment by paying amounts in advance to the developer for construction of the building in which his apartment is to be found. Another vital difference between operational debts and allottees of real estate projects is that, an operational creditor has no interest in or stake in the corporate debtor, unlike the case of an allottee of a real estate project, who is vitally concerned with the financial health of the corporate debtor, for otherwise, the real estate project may not be brought to fruition. Also, in such event, no compensation, nor refund together with interest, which is the other option, will be recoverable from the corporate debtor. One other important distinction is that, in an operational debt, there is no consideration for the time value of money-the consideration of the debt is the goods or services that are either sold or availed of from the operational creditor. Payments made in advance for goods and services are not made to fund manufacture of such goods or provision of such services. Examples given of advance payments being made for turnkey projects and capital goods, where customisation and uniqueness of such goods are important by reason of which advance payments are made, are wholly inapposite as examples vis-a-vis advance payments made

by allottees. In real estate projects, money is raised from the allottee, being raised against consideration for the time value of money. Even the total consideration agreed at a time when the flat/apartment is non-existent or incomplete, is significantly less than the price the buyer would have to pay for a ready/complete flat/apartment, and therefore, he gains the time value of money. Likewise, the developer who benefits from the amounts disbursed also gains from the time value of money. The fact that the allottee makes such payments in instalments which are co-terminus with phases of completion of the real estate project does not any the less make such payments as payments involving "exchange", i.e. advances paid only in order to obtain a flat/apartment. What is predominant, insofar as the real estate developer is concerned, is the fact that such instalment payments are used as a means of finance qua the real estate project. One other vital difference with operational debts is the fact that the documentary evidence for amounts being due and payable by the real estate developer is there in the form of the information provided by the real estate developer compulsorily under RERA. This information, like the information from information utilities under the Code, makes it easy for home buyers/allottees to approach the NCLT under Section 7 of the Code to trigger the Code on the real estate developer's own information given on its webpage as to delay in construction, etc. It is these fundamental differences between the real estate developer and the supplier of goods and services that the legislature has focused upon and included real estate developers as financial debtors. This being the case, it is clear that there cannot be said to be any infraction of equal protection of the laws. [40]

3. The Code is thus a beneficial legislation which can be triggered to put the corporate debtor back on its feet in the interest of unsecured creditors like allottees, who are vitally interested in the financial health of the corporate debtor, so that a replaced management may then carry out the real estate project as originally envisaged and deliver the flat/apartment as soon as

possible and/or pay compensation in the event of late delivery, or non-delivery, or refund amounts advanced together with interest. Thus, applying the Shayara Bano v. Union of India test, it cannot be said that a square peg has been forcibly fixed into a round hole so as to render Section 5(8)(f) manifestly arbitrary i.e. excessive, disproportionate or without adequate determining principle. For the same reason, it cannot be said that Article 19(1)(g) has been infracted and not saved by Article 19(6) as the Amendment Act is made in public interest, and it cannot be said to be an unreasonable restriction on the Petitioner's fundamental right under Article 19(1)(g). Also, there is no infraction of Article 300-A, as no person is deprived of its property without authority of a constitutionally valid law. [45]

4. Allottees/home buyers were included in the main provision, i.e. Section 5(8)(f) with effect from the inception of the Code, the explanation being added in 2018 merely to clarify doubts that had arisen. The Amendment Act to the Code does not infringe Articles 14, 19(1)(g) read with Article 19(6), or 300-A of the Constitution of India. The RERA is to be read harmoniously with the Code, as amended by the Amendment Act. It is only in the event of conflict that the Code will prevail over the RERA. Remedies that are given to allottees of flats/apartments are therefore concurrent remedies, such allottees of flats/apartments being in a position to avail of remedies under the Consumer Protection Act, 1986, RERA as well as the triggering of the Code. Section 5(8)(f) as it originally appeared in the Code being a residuary provision, always subsumed within it allottees of flats/apartments. The explanation together with the deeming fiction added by the Amendment Act is only clarificatory of this position in law. [86]

5. Given the declaration of the constitutional validity of the Amendment Act, it is absolutely necessary that the NCLT and the NCLAT are manned with sufficient members to deal with litigation that may arise under the Code generally, and from the real estate sector in particular. [88]

6. Stay orders granted by this Court to continue until the NCLT takes up each application filed by an allottee/home buyer to decide the same in light of this judgment. Appeals disposed off. [89]

> **Legal Latin Terms Group 12**
>
> manu forti - Forcible entry
>
> mens rea - Guilty mind
>
> nihil dicit - He says nothing
>
> nil - Nothing
>
> nil debet - He owes nothing
>
> nisi prius - Distinguishing the trial court from the appellate court
>
> nolle prosequi - Unwilling to prosecute
>
> nolo contendere - "I will not contest it"; a criminal plea
>
> non - Not
>
> non assumpsit - Plea in defense; that he did not promise
>
> non compos mentis - "Not of sound mind"

33

ROJER MATHEW VS. SOUTH INDIAN BANK LTD. AND ORS. (13.11.2019 – SC)

Relevant Section: Constitution Of India - Article 110; Constitution Of India - Article 323-A; Constitution Of India - Article 323-B; Finance Act, 2017 - Section 184, Insolvency And Bankruptcy Code, 2016 - Section 62, Section 182;

Hon'ble Judges/Coram: Ranjan Gogoi, C.J.I., N.V. Ramana, Dr. D.Y. Chandrachud, Deepak Gupta and Sanjiv Khanna, JJ.

Number of PDF Pages in Original Judgement: 150

Citation: 2019(369)ELT3(S.C.), 2019(15)SCALE615, MANU/SC/1563/2019

Case Note: Constitution- Validity of provision - Section 184 of the Finance Act, 2017 and Articles 110, 323-A and 323-B of Constitution of India, 1950 - In present batch of cases, Petitioners had questioned validity of Part XIV read with 8th and 9th Schedules of Finance Act 2017, as being ex-facie unconstitutional, arbitrary, in colourable exercise of legislative power, and offensive to basic structure of Constitution - Whether 'Finance Act, 2017' insofar as it amended certain other enactments and altered conditions of service of persons manning different Tribunals could be termed as a 'money bill' under Article 110 and consequently was validly enacted - If the answer to the above was in the affirmative then Whether Section

184 of the Finance Act, 2017 was unconstitutional on account of Excessive Delegation - If Section 184 was valid, Whether Tribunal, Appellate Tribunal and other Authorities (Qualifications, Experience and other Conditions of Service of Members) Rules, 2017 were in consonance with Principal Act and various decisions of this Court on functioning of Tribunals - Whether there should be a Single Nodal Agency for administration of all Tribunals - Whether there was a need for conducting a Judicial Impact Assessment of all Tribunals in India - Whether judges of Tribunals set up by Acts of Parliament under Articles 323-A and 323-B of the Constitution can be equated in 'rank' and 'status' with Constitutional functionaries - Whether direct statutory appeals from Tribunals to the Supreme Court ought to be detoured - Whether there was a need for amalgamation of existing Tribunals and setting up of benches.

Stroked down Section 184 of Finance Act, 2017

Facts: The present lead matter was filed by Rojer Mathew, assailing the final judgment and order of the High Court of Kerala. The Petitioner had originally approached the High Court challenging the constitutional validity of Section 13 (5-A) of the Securitisation and Reconstruction of Financial Assets and Enforcement of Securities Interest (SARFAESI) Act, 2002 which permits secured creditors to participate in auction of immoveable property if it remained unsold for want of reserve bid in an earlier auction. Rojer Mathew claimed that the aforementioned provision violated his rights Under Article 300A and Article 14 of the Constitution, besides being in contravention of the Code of Civil Procedure which prohibits mortgagees from participating in auction of immovable property without prior Court permission.

Hon'ble Apex Court held, while striking down Section 184 of Finance Act, 2017

Ranjan Gogoi, C.J.I.

1. It is apparent that the Legislature has not been provided with desired assistance so that it may rectify the anomalies which

arise from provisions of direct appeal to the Supreme Court. Considering that such direct appeals have become serious impediments in the discharge of Constitutional functions by this Court and also affects access to justice for citizens, it is high time that the Union of India, in consultation with either the Law Commission or any other expert body, revisit such provisions under various enactments providing for direct appeals to the Supreme Court against orders of Tribunals, and instead provide appeals to Division Benches of High Courts, if at all necessary. Doing so would have myriad benefits. In addition to increasing affordability of justice and more effective Constitutional adjudication by this Court, it would also provide an avenue for High Court Judges to keep face with contemporaneous evolutions in law, and hence enrich them with adequate experience before they come to this Court. The Union is directed undertake such an exercise expeditiously, preferably within a period of six months at the maximum, and place the findings before Parliament for appropriate action as may be deemed fit.[223]

2. While seeking a 'Judicial Impact Assessment' of all existing Tribunals, counsels for Petitioners/Appellant(s) have underscored the exorbitant pendency before of a number of Tribunals like the CESTAT and ITAT, which they claim affects the very objective of tribunalisation. On the other hand, they also highlight an incongruity wherein numerous Tribunals are hardly seized of any matters, and are exclusively situated in one location.[224]

3. As noted by this Court on numerous occasions, including in Madras Bar Association (2014), although it is the prerogative of the Legislature to set up alternate avenues for dispute resolution to supplement the functioning of existing Courts, it is essential that such mechanisms are equally effective, competent and accessible. Given that jurisdiction of High Courts and District Courts is affected by the constitution of Tribunals, it is necessary that benches of the Tribunals be established across the country. However, owing to the small number of cases, many of these

Tribunals do not have the critical mass of cases required for setting up of multiple benches. On the other hand, it is evident that other Tribunals are pressed for resources and personnel. [225]

4. This 'imbalance' in distribution of case-load and inconsistencies in nature, location and functioning of Tribunals require urgent attention. It is essential that after conducting a Judicial Impact Assessment as directed earlier, such 'niche' Tribunals be amalgamated with others dealing with similar areas of law, to ensure effective utilisation of resources and to facilitate access to justice. [226]

5. Union is directed to rationalise and amalgamate the existing Tribunals depending upon their case-load and commonality of subject-matter after conducting a Judicial Impact Assessment, in line with the recommendation of the Law Commission of India in its 272nd Report. Additionally, the Union must ensure that, at the very least, circuit benches of all Tribunals are set up at the seats of all major jurisdictional High Courts. [227]

6. The issue and question of Money Bill, as defined Under Article 110(1) of the Constitution, and certification accorded by the Speaker of the Lok Sabha in respect of Part-XIV of the Finance Act, 2017 is referred to a larger Bench. Section 184 of the Finance Act, 2017 does not suffer from excessive delegation of legislative functions as there are adequate principles to guide framing of delegated legislation, which would include the binding dictums of this Court. The Tribunal, Appellate Tribunal and other Authorities (Qualifications, Experience and other Conditions of Service of Members) Rules, 2017 suffer from various infirmities. These Rules formulated by the Central Government under Section 184 of the Finance Act, 2017 being contrary to the parent enactment and the principles envisaged in the Constitution as interpreted by this Court, are hereby struck down in entirety. The Central Government is accordingly directed to re-formulate the Rules strictly in conformity and in accordance with the principles delineated by this Court in R.K.

Jain, L. Chandra Kumar, Madras Bar Association and Gujarat Urja Vikas Ltd. conjointly read with the observations made in the earlier part of this decision. The new set of Rules to be formulated by the Central Government shall ensure non-discriminatory and uniform conditions of service, including assured tenure, keeping in mind the fact that the Chairperson and Members appointed after retirement and those who are appointed from the Bar or from other specialised professions/services, constitute two separate and distinct homogeneous classes. It would be open to the Central Government to provide in the new set of Rules that the Presiding Officers or Members of the Statutory Tribunals shall not hold 'rank' and 'status' equivalent to that of the Judges of the Supreme Court or High Courts, as the case may be, only on the basis of drawing equal salary or other perquisites. There is a need-based requirement to conduct 'Judicial Impact Assessment' of all the Tribunals referable to the Finance Act, 2017 so as to analyse the ramifications of the changes in the framework of Tribunals as provided under the Finance Act, 2017. Thus, it is appropriate to issue a writ of mandamus to the Ministry of Law and Justice to carry out such 'Judicial Impact Assessment' and submit the result of the findings before the competent legislative authority. The Central Government in consultation with the Law Commission of India or any other expert body shall revisit the provisions of the statutes referable to the Finance Act, 2017 or other Acts as listed in para 174 of this order and place appropriate proposals before the Parliament for consideration of the need to remove direct appeals to the Supreme Court from orders of Tribunals. A decision in this regard by the Union of India shall be taken within six months. The Union Government shall carry out an appropriate exercise for amalgamation of existing Tribunals adopting the test of homogeneity of the subject matters to be dealt with and thereafter constitute adequate number of Benches commensurate with the existing and anticipated volume of work.[228]

7. As the Tribunal, Appellate Tribunal and other Authorities (Qualification, Experience and other Conditions of Service of Members) Rules, 2017 have been struck down and several directions have been issued vide the majority judgment for framing of fresh set of Rules, present Court, as an interim order, direct that appointments to the Tribunal/Appellate Tribunal and the terms and conditions of appointment shall be in terms of the respective statutes before the enactment of the Finance Bill, 2017. However, liberty is granted to the Union of India to seek modification of this order after they have framed fresh Rules in accordance with the majority judgment. However, in case any additional benefits concerning the salaries and emoluments have been granted under the Finance Act, they shall not be withdrawn and will be continued. These would equally apply to all new members.[229]

8. The present batch of matters is accordingly disposed of.[230]

Dr. D.Y. Chandrachud, J.

9. Part XIV of the Finance Act 2017 could not have been enacted in the form of a Money Bill. The Rules which have been framed pursuant of the Rule making power Under Section 184 are held to be unconstitutional. However, since during the pendency of these proceedings, certain steps were taken in pursuance of the interim orders and appointments have been made, we direct that those appointments shall not be affected by the declaration of unconstitutionality. The terms and conditions governing the personnel so appointed shall however abide by the parent enactments. Upon the declaration of unconstitutionality, the conditions specified in all corresponding aspects in the parent enactments shall continue to operate.[334]

10. This Court has repeatedly emphasised the need for setting up an independent statutory body to oversee the working of tribunals. Despite the directions issued by this Court in Chandra Kumar nearly two decades ago, no action has been taken by the legislature to put in place an umbrella organisation which

would be tasked with addressing the drawbacks of the system to which we have adverted above. The lack of a single authority to ensure competence and uniform service conditions has led to a fragmented tribunal system that defeats the purpose for which the system was constituted. Moreover, the co-ordinating authority for all tribunals must be the Department of Justice. Vesting that function in individual ministries has led to haphazard evolution of the tribunal structure, besides posing serious dangers to the independence of tribunals.[335]

11. It is imperative that an overarching statutory organisation be constituted through legislative intervention to oversee the working of tribunals. We recommend the constitution of an independent statutory body called the "National Tribunals Commission"39 to oversee the selection process of members, criteria for appointment, salaries and allowances, introduction of common eligibility criteria, for removal of Chairpersons and Members as also for meeting the requirement of infrastructural and financial resources. The legislation should aim at prescribing uniform service conditions for members. The Commission should comprise the following members: (i) Three serving judges of the Supreme Court of India nominated by the Chief Justice of India; (ii) Two serving Chief Justices or judges of the High Court nominated by the Chief Justice of India; (iii) Two members to be nominated by the Central Government from amongst officers holding at least the rank to a Secretary to the Union Government: one of them shall be the Secretary to the Department of Justice who will be the ex-officio convener; and (iv) Two independent expert members to be nominated by the Union government in consultation with the Chief Justice of India.[336]

12. The senior-most among the Judges nominated by the Chief Justice of India shall be designated as the Chairperson of the NTC.[337]

13. While the setting up of the NTC is within the competence of the legislature, it must be ensured that the guidelines that have been

laid down by this Court to ensure the independence and efficient functioning of the tribunal system in India are observed. The independence of judicial tribunals is an inviolable feature of the basic structure of the Constitution. The procedure of selection, appointment, removal of members and prescription of the service conditions of tribunal members determine the independence of the tribunals. As we have held, in preserving the independence of the tribunals as a facet of judicial independence, the adjudicatory body must be robust: subservient to none and accountable to the need to render justice in the context of specialized adjudication. This is reflected in the need for vigilance in guarding the independence of courts and tribunals. [338]

14. Competence, professionalism and specialisation are indispensable facets of a robust tribunal system designed to deliver specialised justice. The Commission must be vested with the power to oversee the administration of all tribunals established under the enactments of Parliament to ensure the adequate manning of the tribunals with the infrastructure and staff required to meet the exigencies of the system. The Union government should also consider formulating a law to ensure the constitution of an All India Tribunal Service governing the recruitment and conditions of service of the non-adjudicatory personnel for tribunals. At present, the administrative staff of the tribunals is by and large brought on deputation. The tribunals are woefully short of an adequate complement of trained administrative personnel. Hence, there is an urgent need to set up an All India Tribunal Service in the interests of the effective functioning of the tribunal system. Though the present judgment analyses the ambit of the word "only" in Article 110(1) and the interpretation of Sub-clauses (a) to (g) of Clause (1) of Article 110 and concludes that Part XIV of the Finance Act 2017 could not have been validly enacted as a Money Bill. The qualifications of members to tribunals constitute an essential legislative function and cannot be delegated. Tribunals have been conceptualized as specialized bodies with domain-specific knowledge expertise. Indispensable to this specialized adjudicatory function is the

selection of members trained in their discipline. Keeping this in mind, the prescription of qualifications for members of tribunals is a legislative function in its most essential character. The qualifications for appointment to adjudicatory bodies determine the character of the body. The adjudicatory tribunals are intended to fulfil the objects of legislation enacted by Parliament, be it in the area of consumer protection, environmental adjudication, industrial disputes and in diverse aspects of economic regulation. Defining the qualifications necessary for appointment of members constitutes the core, the very essence of the tribunal. This is an essential legislative function and cannot be delegated to the Rule making authority of the central government. It is for the legislature to define the conditions which must be fulfilled for appointment after assessing the need for domain specific knowledge.[339]

Deepak Gupta, J.

15. The decision of the Hon'ble Speaker of the House of People under Article 110 (3) of the Constitution is not beyond judicial review. If two views are possible then there can be no manner of doubt that the view of the Speaker must prevail. Keeping in view the lack of clarity as to what constitutes a Money Bill, the issue as to whether Part XIV of the Finance Act, 2017, is a Money Bill or not may be referred to a larger bench.[357]

16. There can be no doubt that Parliament is not expected to deal with all matters and it can delegate certain "non-essential" matters to the executive. Every condition need not be laid down by the Legislature.[358]

17. A 7-Judge Bench of this Court in Re Article 143, Constitution of India and Delhi Laws Act (1912) etc. held that, the legislature cannot be expected to legislate on all issues and has the power to delegate non-essential functions to a delegatee. At the same time, a close reading of the judgment indicates that it was clearly held that the "essential legislative functions" cannot be delegated. There can be no quarrel with the proposition that

delegation of non-essential legislative functions can be done. Even to this there is a caveat. The legislature must have control and functional powers over the delegatee. One of the known methods of exercising such powers is for the delegatee to place the rules/orders passed by it in exercise of powers delegated to it before the legislature. There should always be legislative control over delegated legislation. [360]

18. An analysis of Section 184 clearly indicates that the Parliament has delegated to the Central Government the power to make Rules to provide for the qualifications, appointment, term of office, salaries and allowances, resignation, removal and other terms and conditions of the Chairpersons/Members of the tribunals. The issue before us is whether by doing so Parliament has delegated "essential legislative functions" and whether Parliament has retained any control. [365]

19. Present Court in the present case dealing with the appointment of Chairpersons/Members to various Tribunals. They are enjoined upon to discharge a constitutional function of delivering justice to the people. What should be the essential qualifications and attributes of persons selected to man such high posts is, an essential part of legislative functions. Constitution could not have provided that the qualifications of the Judges of the Supreme Court of India or of the High Courts could be fixed by the Government. If these tribunals are to replace the High Courts, why should the same principles not apply to them. Laying down the qualifications of the persons eligible to hold these high posts was an essential aspect of the legislation keeping in view the importance of the tribunals, the importance of Rule of law and the importance of an independent and fearless judiciary. [358]

20. As far as providing the qualifications for appointment are concerned, these qualifications have to be provided in the legislation and could not be delegated. However, as far as the other terms and conditions such as pay and allowances are concerned, these can be delegated. [367]

21. For the sake of argument, even if it was to be said that laying down the qualifications is not an essential function then also, in view

of the law laid down by this Court, the guidelines should have been found in the legislation itself. It is paradoxical that there are no guidelines for the essential qualifications, even though there are some guidelines with regard to the terms and conditions of services of Chairpersons/Members of the Tribunals. [368]

22. The previous enactments were repealed in so far as matters covered by Part XIV of the Finance Act are concerned. Therefore, it cannot be expected that the delegatee would again refer to the repealed enactments to seek the guidelines for fixing the terms and conditions, etc. of those to be appointed as Chairpersons/Members. If we exclude the judgments of this Court and the terms and conditions laid down in the repealed enactments then there are no guidelines whatsoever left for the delegatee to fall back on. The Finance Act provides no guidelines in this regard. It is absolutely silent with regard to the qualification, the eligibility criteria, experience etc. required for those who are to be appointed as Chairpersons/Members of the Tribunals. These powers have been delegated to the government. [370]

23. There being no guidelines, unfettered and unguided powers have been vested in the delegatee and, therefore, in my opinion, there is excessive delegation. As such Section 184 of the Finance Act, 2017 insofar as it delegates the powers to lay down the qualifications of Chairperson, Vice-Chairperson, Chairman, Vice-Chairman, President, Vice-President, Presiding Officer or Member of the Tribunal, Appellate Tribunal or, as the case may be, other Authorities as specified in column (2) of the Eighth Schedule, suffers from the vice of excessive delegation and is accordingly struck down. [371]

24. There are various reasons why there should be one nodal agency. Tribunals are facing many problems like lack of manpower, very few benches, vacancies lying unfilled for long period, financial dependence on the department which may be litigating before the tribunal etc. These are ills which can be avoided if Tribunals fall under one umbrella organisation. One umbrella organisation will be better equipped to understand the problems faced by all

the Tribunals. This could lead to standardization of Tribunals and a uniform approach to the needs of each tribunal. A large number of tribunals, especially those cast with the duty of discharging adjudicatory functions have been constituted with a view to replace the courts and in many cases the jurisdiction earlier exercised by the High Courts has been vested in such tribunals. It is, therefore, imperative that these tribunals must be manned by persons of impeccable integrity, high intellect and having vast experience in the field in which they will exercise jurisdiction. These tribunals also must have functional autonomy. This cannot be achieved unless there is a nodal body which shall look after the administrative needs of the tribunals. For more than 2 decades the Government has not thought it fit to comply with the 7-Judge Bench judgment of this Court in L. Chandra Kumar. These matters cannot be permitted to linger on indefinitely. Therefore, in my view, a direction must be given to the Government to set up a single nodal agency within a period of 6 months from today till which time the present system may continue. Merely giving financial autonomy to the tribunals will not do away with the need of having one common umbrella organisation to supervise all the tribunals.[375]

25. Even without carrying out any judicial impact assessment it is clear, as held in Madras Bar Association, 2010 that, tribunals in India have unfortunately not achieved full independence. When tribunals are established, they depend upon the sponsoring department for funds, infrastructure and even space for functioning. Administrative members of the tribunal are, more often than not, drawn from this department. This strikes at the very root of judicial independence because the biggest litigant or stakeholder itself becomes part and parcel of the adjudicating body which is supposed to be free, independent and fearless.[376]

26. An attempt should be made to do away with filing of first appeal as a matter of right to the Supreme Court. At present, at least 2 dozen statues provide for appeals directly to the Supreme Court. The Supreme Court becomes a Court of first appeal which is highly avoidable. If the jurisdiction of the High Courts

is bypassed by providing for appeals directly to the Supreme Court, soon a stage will come when we will have no High Court Judges who would have heard matters in various jurisdictions. It would be virtually impossible for them to handle such matters in the Supreme Court where the tenure of a Judge is on an average only about 4 years.[390]

27. The Judicial Impact Assessment Committee can also after assessment recommend that some tribunal(s) should be wound up and the jurisdiction of that tribunal(s) be given back to civil courts or to the High Courts or to some other tribunal. It can also suggest the merger of two or more tribunals.[391]

28. The next issue is who should carry out the judicial impact assessment. The Judicial Impact Assessment Committee should comprise of two retired judges of the Supreme Court, the senior being the Chairperson of the Committee, and one retired Chief Justice of a High Court all three to be nominated by the Chief Justice of India. Out of the three at least two should have been the Chairperson or members of tribunals. Two members of the Executive, not below the rank of Secretary, to the Government of India, one from the Ministry of Law and Justice and one from some other branch can also be members but these members should be appointed in consultation with the Chief Justice of India.[392]

29. The last issue is whether there should be a Commission or a body to oversee the appointment of members of various tribunals. It is necessary to have such a Commission which is itself an independent body manned by honest and competent persons. This body is required to select those persons who man the specialised tribunals in terms of the law laid down in various judgments of this Court.[393]

30. Serving Judges of the Supreme Court or the Chief Justice of the High Courts are already overburdened and have no time to spare. It would be much better, if they could spend their time and energy in filling up the vacancies in the High Courts rather than venturing into the field of tribunals.[394]

31. Having a very large committee would not serve the purpose. A smaller committee comprising of competent people is a better solution and, such commission should comprise of 2 retired Supreme Court Judges with the senior most being the Chairman and one retired Chief Justice of High Court to be appointed by the Chief Justice of India. There must be one member representing the executive to be nominated by the Central Government from amongst officers holding the rank of Secretary to the Government of India or equivalent. This member shall be the ex-officio convener. One expert member can be co-opted by the by full time members. This expert member must have expertise and experience in the field/jurisdiction covered by the tribunal to which appointments are to be made.[395]

Legal Latin Terms Group 13

non est factum - "It is not his deed"

non obstante - Notwithstanding

non sequitur - "It does not follow"

nota bene - Note well; take notice

nudum pactum - A bare agreement lacking consideration

nul tort - "No wrong done"

nulla bona - "No good"

nunc pro tunc - "Now for then"

obiter dictum - A remark made by a court that is not central to a main issue in the case.

onus probandi - Burden of Proof

opus - Work or labor

34

LMJ International Ltd. and Ors. vs. Sleepwell Industries Co. Ltd. (20.02.2019 – SC)

Relevant Section: Arbitration And Conciliation Act, 1996 - Section 49; Section 48, Insolvency and Bankruptcy Code, 2016 - Section 10

Hon'ble Judges/Coram: A.M. Khanwilkar and Ajay Rastogi, JJ.

Number of PDF Pages in Original Judgement: 19

Citation: 2019(2)ARBLR98(SC), [2019]150CLA451(SC), 2019(3)CTC93, 123(1)CWN458, 2019(2)RCR(Civil)468, 2019(3)SCALE703, (2019)5SCC302, MANU/SC/0251/2019

Case Note: Arbitration - Foreign award - Enforcement of - Parties had entered into separate contracts for sale of Non Basmati Parboiled Rice, on terms and conditions specified in contracts - Some dispute arose regarding inferior quality of rice and non-release of payment - Respondent, invoked arbitration Clause - Arbitral Tribunal passed two separate awards in relation to concerned contracts - Respondent filed execution cases, before High Court for enforcement of foreign arbitral awards - Single judge held that subject foreign awards were deemed to be decrees and hence enforceable, whilst rejecting objections of Petitioner with regard to maintainability of execution petition - Hence, present petition - Whether impugned order pertaining to enforcement of foreign award warrant any interference.

Petition Dismissed

Facts: The parties had entered into separate contracts for sale of Non Basmati Parboiled Rice, foreign origin, on the terms and conditions specified in the contracts. Some dispute arose regarding the inferior quality of rice and non-release of the payment towards the invoices raised by the seller in respect of certain shipment, which eventually became the subject matter of arbitration proceedings. The Respondent, invoked the arbitration Clause. Arbitral Tribunal passed two separate awards in relation to the concerned contracts. Respondent filed execution cases, before the High Court for enforcement of the foreign arbitral awards. The Single judge held that subject foreign awards were deemed to be decrees and hence enforceable, whilst rejecting the objections of the Petitioner in both the cases with regard to the maintainability of the execution petition.

Hon'ble Apex Court held, while dismissing the petition it is held:

i. The grounds urged by the Petitioner to question the enforceability of the subject foreign awards are untenable, not being within the purview of Section 48 of the Act. The High Court had considered every aspect of the grounds urged by the Petitioner and the view so expressed by the High Court in reference to each of the points considered by it was a possible view. The High Court had correctly noted the limited scope for interference in the matter of foreign awards under Section 48 of the Act, keeping in view the principles enunciated by this Court. The High Court had justly noted that the attempt of the Petitioner was to call upon the executing court to have a re-look at the award. That could not be countenanced. All the relevant documents submitted to buttress the claim of the Respondent before the Arbitral Tribunal, had been adverted to in the award and the findings reached in the award were based on the interpretation and meaning given to the said documents. [16]

ii. The Arbitral Tribunal had considered all aspects of the matter and even if it had committed any error, the same could, at best, be a matter for correction by way of appeal to be resorted to on grounds as may be permissible under the English Law, by which the subject arbitration proceedings were governed. [17]

Legal Latin Terms Group 14

ore tenus - By word of mouth

pari delicto - In equal fault

pari passu - By equal progress

pater familias - Father of the family

peculium - Private property

pendens - "Pending"

pendente lite - Pending the suit, during litigation

per annum - Annual, by the year

per capita - By the head, equally shared

per contra - "In opposition"

per curiam - "By the court"

35

STANDARD CHARTERED BANK VS. MSTC LIMITED (21.01.2020 – SC)

Relevant Section: Recovery Of Debts And Bankruptcy, Insolvency Resolution And Bankruptcy Of Individuals And Partnership Firms Act, 1993 - Section 22(2)(e)

Hon'ble Judges/Coram: Rohinton Fali Nariman and V. Ramasubramanian, JJ.

Number of PDF Pages in Original Judgement: 14

Citation: I(2020)BC524(SC), 2020-2-LW377, 2020 (1) WLN 156 (SC), MANU/SC/0073/2020

Case Note: Company - Review application - Delay in filing - Sections 20, 22(1) and 34 of Recovery of Debts and Bankruptcy Act, 1993 and Rule 5A of Debt Recovery Tribunal Rules, 1993 - Receivables Purchase Agreement was executed between Appellant and Respondent- Government Company - Export Insurance Policy was obtained under which Insurance Company agreed to indemnify Respondent and Appellant in event of default in payment of foreign buyers - Appellant had lodged claim with said Insurance Company which, however, was repudiated - Application was filed by Appellant stating that given admissions contained in balance sheet of relevant years of Respondent-Company, certain sum was owed by Respondent to Appellant - Said application was allowed by DRT -

Appeal was filed by Respondent-Company against said order before Appellate Tribunal - While appeal was pending, review application was filed before DRT by the Respondent-Company - In meanwhile, application was made to condone delay in filing review petition before DRT - Said review petition was dismissed by DRT holding that Section 5 of Limitation Act, 1963 was held not to be applicable to review petitions that were filed under Rule 5A of Rules - Further plea to exclude time taken under Section 14 of Limitation Act, 1963 was also dismissed by DRT - Writ petition was filed before High Court - High Court set aside judgment of DRT, condoned delay in filing of review application - Hence, present appeal - Whether High Court erred in setting aside judgment of DRT, condoned delay in filing of review application.

Facts: A Receivables Purchase Agreement was executed between the Appellant and Government Company-Respondent whereunder receivables from overseas buyers in respect of invoices raised by the Respondent against foreign buyers were purchased by the Appellant. An Export Insurance Policy was obtained by these parties under which the Insurance Company agreed to indemnify the Respondent and the Appellant in the event of default in payment of foreign buyers. The Appellant had lodged a claim with the said Insurance Company which, however, was repudiated. An application was filed by the Appellant stating that given the admissions contained in the balance sheet of the relevant years of the Respondent-Company, a sum was owed by the Respondent to the Appellant. This application was allowed by the DRT. An appeal was filed by the Respondent-Company against the said order before the DRAT. While the appeal was pending, Review Application was filed before the DRT by the Respondent-Company after the appeal that was lodged earlier in point of time was withdrawn by the Respondent-Company. In the meanwhile, an application was made to condone a delay in filing the review petition before the DRT, the period of limitation under Rule 5A of the Debt Recovery Tribunal Rules, 1993. This review petition was dismissed by the DRT by holding that Section 5 of the Limitation Act, 1963 was held not to be applicable to review petitions that were filed under Rule 5A of the Rules. A writ petition was filed before the High Court. The High Court set aside the judgment of the DRT, condoned the delay in filing of the review application itself, and restored the review application to the file.

Appeal Allowed

Hon'ble Apex Court held, while allowing the appeal:

i. The peremptory language of Rule 5A would also make it clear that beyond thirty days there is no power to condone delay. Rule 5A was added with a longer period within which to file a review petition. This period was cut down, by amendment to thirty days. From this two things were clear one, whether in the original or unamended provision, there was no separate power to condone delay, as was contained in Section 20(3) of the Act and second, that the period of sixty days was considered too long and cut down to thirty days thereby evincing an intention that review petitions, if they were to be filed, should be within a shorter period of limitation - otherwise they would not be maintainable. [14]

ii. Section 22(1) of the Act makes it clear that the Tribunal and the Appellate Tribunal shall not be bound by the procedure laid down by the Code of Civil Procedure, making it clear thereby that Order 47 Rule 7 would not apply to the Tribunal. Also, in view of Section 20, which applies to all applications that may be made, including applications for review, and orders being made therein being subject to appeal, it was a little difficult to appreciate how Order 47 Rule 7 could apply at all, given that Section 20 of the RDB Act was part of a complete and exhaustive code. Section 34 of the Act makes it clear that the 1993 Act, would have overriding effect over any other law for the time being in force, which includes the Code of Civil Procedure. The High Court, in holding that no appeal would be maintainable against the dismissal of the review petition, and that therefore a writ petition would be maintainable, was clearly in error on this count also. [16]

Synopsis

This book is related to the Supreme Court of India's Leading Case Laws on Insolvency & Bankruptcy Code 2016.

Book will be useful for Advocates, Insolvency Professionals, Chartered Accountants, Company Secretaries, Corporate Applicants, Corporate Debtors, Corporates, MNCs, IPAs, IPEs, NCLT, NCLAT, DRT & DRAT, High Courts & Supreme Court Librarians, Entrepreneurs, Individuals, Consultants, Valuers, Law Students & Law School Faculties,

This book is containing a synopsis of 35 leading causes of the Apex Court. Following points are given for each leading case.

1. Name of the Case i. e. Cause title
2. Relevant Sections discussed in the case
3. Hon'ble Judges/Coram of the case
4. Number of PDF Pages in Original Judgement of the case
5. All available Citations of the case
6. Case Note with appeal allowed/ dismissed or disposed off
7. Facts of the case
8. Hon'ble Apex Court's findings, while dismissing/allowing or disposing off the appeal
9. Ratio Decidendi if any.

List of some important videos & TV shows on Law & EXIM by Adv. Jayprakash Somani on his YouTube Channel 'jaysomani64'

Law Videos:

1. SLP in Supreme Court / Special Leave Petitions in the Supreme Court of India
2. Transfer of Civil & Criminal Cases by the Supreme Court of India / Transfer of Matrimonial Cases
3. Appealat Jurisdiction of the Supreme Court of India
4. Jurisdictions of the Supreme Court of India
5. Public Interest Litigation in the Supreme Court of India / PIL in Supreme Court
6. Article 32 Writ Petitions in the Supreme Court of India
7. Bail Matters Top 10 Supreme Court Cases
8. FIR Quashing in High Court & Supreme Court
9. Bail & Anticipatory Bail Matters in Supreme Court
10. Insolvency & Bankruptcy Matters in the Supreme Court
11. Insolvency & Bankruptcy Code 2016 Part 1
12. Insolvency & Bankruptcy Code 2016 Part 2
13. Insolvency & Bankruptcy Code 2016 Part 3

14. Corporate Liquidation Process
15. Supreme Court Rules & Procedures Webinar of 2.5 hours on Zoom
16. RDDBFI Act, 1993 (Introduction)
17. The Indian Contact Act 1872
18. Negotiable Instruments Act (Introduction)
19. How to avoid matrimonial disputes & some more videos

EXIM Videos:

1. Yes, I can do Import Export Business Easily! 36 points excellent video in Hindi
2. Yes, I can do Import Export Business Easily! 36 points excellent video in English
3. Import Export Business – Hindi video
4. Import Export Business - English video
5. Export-Import Marathi TV Interview
6. Scope for Commerce Students in International Business- TV Show
7. Scope for Management Student in International Business- TV Show
8. Scope for Engineering Students in International Business – TV Show
9. Women in International Business- TV Show
10. How to do Import Export Business Successfully!'
11. Where one can get full information on Import Export Business?
12. What to do import & export?
13. Import Export Workshop/ Training/Course/ Diploma

14. How to Start Import Export Business & How to grow it. Live Webinar
15. Success Stories & Failure Stories in Import & Export Business
16. For MSME Scope in Export & Import...
17. Exports In Agri. & Food Products – English & some more videos

List of Adv. Jayprakash Somani's Upcoming Books

1. Scope in Agri and Food Products Export From India
2. Supreme Court Case Laws on 'Bail and Anticipatory Bail Matters'
3. Scope in Textile and Apparel Products Export From India
4. Supreme Court Case Laws on 'Companies Act, 2013
5. Scope in Pharma Products Export From India
6. Supreme Court Case Laws on 'Arbitration and Conciliation Act, 1996'
7. Scope in Engineering Product Export From India.
8. Supreme Court Case Laws on 'Transfer of Property Act, 1882'
9. Scope in Different Services Export From India
10. Supreme Court Case Laws on 'Recovery of Debts due to Banks and Financial Institutions Act, 1993'
11. Scope in Handloom & Handicraft Products Export From India.

www.ingramcontent.com/pod-product-compliance
Lightning Source LLC
Chambersburg PA
CBHW031048180526
45163CB00002BA/736